The Art and Science of String Performance

Contents

CHAPTER ONE

CHAPTER TWO

CHAPTER THREE

CHAPTER FOUR

CHAPTER FIVE

CHAPTER SIX

CHAPTER SEVEN

CHAPTER EIGHT

CHAPTER NINE

CHAPTER NINE *(Continued)*

CHAPTER TEN

CHAPTER ELEVEN

CHAPTER TWELVE

CHAPTER THIRTEEN

CHAPTER FOURTEEN

CHAPTER FIFTEEN

CHAPTER SIXTEEN

CHAPTER SEVENTEEN

CHAPTER EIGHTEEN

CHAPTER NINETEEN

CHAPTER TWENTY

CHAPTER TWENTY-ONE

CHAPTER TWENTY-TWO

Foreword

FOREWORD

As a result of four decades of lecturing and conducting workshops in America and abroad for string teachers and performers, Dr. Applebaum has catalogued the most frequently asked questions ranging from the very basic to the most advanced.

Dr. Applebaum has spent many years conferring with the greatest concert artists of our time, discussing and analyzing the string instruments from the holding of the instruments and bows to the most advanced complexities of technic and interpretation. Most of the exercises throughout this book can be adapted to the cello and bass.

We have tried to make this work interesting and comprehensive, yet readily understandable by students and teachers, professional performers and other lovers of the art of string playing. Therefore, a conversational style has been employed, rather than a more formal prose. It will serve as a basic study guide and a life-long, handy reference.

THE PUBLISHERS

The Basic Principles of String Playing

Q. What suggestions would you make as to just how to hold the violin or viola?

A. There are various ways to teach the holding of the instrument all of which can produce good results. At the very beginning, some teachers favor the guitar position. The player's physique, the length of the arm, and the height of the neck are to be carefully considered. Here are some basic principles.

The violin might well rest on the collar bone midway between the front of the body and the left shoulder, and held as high as the upper lip with the tip of the nose in line with the scroll.

The side of the first finger contacts the neck of the violin or viola a bit above the base knuckle. The thumb contacts the neck slightly above the first crease, more toward the tip of the thumb. Since this is a variable, the thumb may contact the neck at the crease or slightly above or below, depending on the size of the thumb.

The thumb may be placed about one or one-half inch from the nut or the end of the neck. There must always be an open space between the thumb and the first finger under the neck.

The hand and forearm should form a reasonably straight line. The heel (or the palm of the hand) should not be permitted to contact the underside of the neck.

The left elbow is placed under the violin so that the elbow joint is approximately under the center of the violin. Let us call this the neutral position. This varies somewhat, depending upon the size of the left arm and the string that is being played.

Q. What is the best way for a player to stand while playing the violin or viola?

A. The feet should be about ten to twelve inches apart. The performer should be able to balance the weight between both legs and should be able to transfer the body weight from one foot to the other.

I do object to having all the weight placed on the same foot at all times. If a choice must be made, however, the weight should be on the left foot rather than on the right foot. Many teachers, in fact, suggest that the weight should be applied to the left foot and the right foot be slightly forward.

Q. Do you permit the violin to rest on the shoulder when holding the instrument?

A. Many artists do. The violin is then held with the head and the shoulder. Beginning students may find it easier to hold the violin in this way.

Q. Is there another way?

A. Yes, where the violin is balanced between the collar bone and the jaw bone with the head applying a light pressure. This head pressure is applied lightly only when shifts are made. When one remains in the position or if one holds a long note in any one position, head pressure should be practically eliminated.

Q. Which method is more successful when teaching young children?

A. Most young beginners might be better off supporting the instrument with the head and shoulder. Many players, however, are very successful by having the violin rest on the collar bone, with the left hand assuming a bit more of the responsibility in holding or balancing the violin or viola.

Q. Do you approve of the shoulder pad?

A. Here, opinions are divided. Some of my close friends, teachers and famous soloists do not approve of any shoulder pad at all, not even for students with long necks, feeling that they can learn to balance the violin between the collar bone and the jaw.

Q. But is this not more difficult for beginning students?

A. Yes. I think that all students who enter into a string class should have a thin powder puff or thin rubber sponge placed on the instrument just to make it more comfortable and to prevent slipping. This is, of course, up to the teacher.

On the other hand, teachers with a great variety of students are more liberal about the use of the shoulder pad.

Students with long necks are likely to fare better with a shoulder pad. If possible, the pad should touch the edges and not the back of the instrument.

Q. How high should the violin be held?

A. I prefer to have the scroll held as high as the tip of the nose. This brings the violin slightly above the shoulder.

Q. Why above and not on the shoulder level?

A. When the violin is held above the shoulder level, the student, as time goes on, will feel more comfortable in this position. Thus, the violin is more inclined toward the player's neck and collar bone (or neck and shoulder) relieving some of the weight that otherwise would be applied to the left hand.

But there is another factor. When one holds the violin a bit above the shoulder, the left arm can remain in that position longer without tiring. When the violin is held below the shoulder level, there is a tendency for the elbow to come very close to, or even touch the body. The entire arm is so constructed that once the violin is held above the shoulder the student can more easily experience a sensation of the arm actually resting on an imaginary shelf. This sensation cannot be felt when the violin is held below shoulder level.

Q. What sort of chin rest do you recommend?

A. There are so many kinds that each student must decide which one is best. I prefer a larger chin rest with a flatter surface that is not hollowed out so much. If possible, it is good to use a chin rest that is equal on both sides of the tail piece where the chin rest fastens around the tail piece.

If you use one that is fastened to the left of the tail piece, make sure that it is not too tight. Otherwise, it can warp the rib of the instrument. Students must decide for themselves which chin rest is best. The only criteria are comfort and ease in performance.

Q. How far under the instrument should the left elbow be placed?

A. The left elbow is a variable and can swing more or less under the instrument, depending on the string to be played.

With the bass and the cello, the left elbow varies according to the different heights.

Q. Should the left elbow always be kept in the same place?

A. No. The left elbow is a variable, and, if a more percussive type of fingering is required, the elbow may be brought more to the right so that the player will be in a better position to use more of the tip of the finger. For legato passages that are expressive in character, using more of the flesh of the fingers is an advantage because it is conducive to a warmer type of vibrato.

The general rule that I like to follow is that there is a relationship between the left elbow and the fourth finger. I think the left elbow should be directly under the tip of the fourth finger, or it should be reasonably under the tip of the fourth finger. Now, if you are playing the violin on the E string, the elbow would have to pivot a little. If you are playing on the G string, the elbow would have to move a little to the right to be directly under the fourth finger.

Q. Would that also apply to the upper positions?

A. Yes. No matter what position you are in, I like to feel that the left elbow is directly under the fourth finger.

Q. How should the left wrist be placed?

A. That is also a variable, depending on the passage to be played. The general rule is that the left wrist should form a rather straight line with the hand and forearm.

Q. What exceptions are there? How do you alter the position of the wrist in relation to the forearm?

A. The left wrist may bend inward toward the neck for certain passages. For example:

For advanced players

R. Kreutzer

Another example where the left wrist will not necessarily form a straight line is when we play in the half position, when we play certain chords (particulary four voice chords), or when we play in the very high positions. The wrist will then tend to curve outward for more accurate finger action.

Q. What do you consider the ideal way to hold the violin?

A. The violin should be held in such a manner that the whole forearm unit (that is, the forearm to the fingertips) should be able to move up and down the fingerboard with great freedom and speed.

Q. How far above the fingerboard should the fingers be when they leave the string?

A. That depends on the speed of the passage. The faster we play, the closer the fingertips should be to the string. If we play very slowly, the fingers may come up a bit higher. The only set rule is that in the beginning; elementary students should not lift their fingers too high. The other rule is that in the very fast passages the player is hindered by not allowing the finger to remain close to the fingerboard.

Q. In the first position, should the base knuckle of the first finger touch the neck? There seems to be differences of opinion.

A. For the beginner I feel strongly that the base knuckle of the first finger should contact the neck lightly, not pinching the neck, but certainly in contact. We then have the right side of the thumb and the base knuckle of the first finger in contact with the neck, thus offering greater security to the beginner.

Q. Does the advanced player have to do this?

A. The advanced player will know just when to leave the neck and when to contact the neck. Certainly for the vibrato, it is desirable for this base knuckle to leave the neck.

Q. What position should the player be in when it is permitted for the base knuckle of the first finger to leave the neck?

A. That again is a variable, depending on the hand itself. But a good general rule is that it should be at least up to the third or fourth positions.

Q. What suggestions do you have for the setting of the fingers on the fingerboard?

A. For the first finger, the general rule might be that once the finger is set on the string the fingernail should face the player and that the tip of the thumb more or less should be facing the ceiling. However, the tip of the thumb might also incline slightly toward the scroll.

For the second finger, the fingernail will not face the player, but will be more inclined to face to the left of the player's face.

The third finger will incline even more to the left and the same with the fourth finger, even a bit more to the left.

Q. When the fingers are placed on a string, do they contact the string in the center of the finger?

A. No. Most of the time, for technical convenience, the tips of the fingers should be placed a bit to the left of center. In other words, more of the finger will be closer to the next higher string.

Q. What is a good way to check the correct setting of the fingers of the left hand?

A. One way is to place all the fingers on a string and still be able to sound the next higher open string while the fingers remain down. Another way is to be able to place the first and fourth down simultaneously on two different strings: the first on a lower string and the fourth on the next higher string. By so doing, the player will be ready to play an octave. The hand must feel quite relaxed with both fingers remaining down.

You must always bear in mind that the role of the thumb is to counteract the downward weight of the fingers. There should be as little side pressure on the neck as possible. The left thumb must never clutch the fingerboard or neck.

Q. When a person is in the habit of clutching, what would you suggest?

A. This is an exercise which might help. Place the four fingers on the D string, and with the fingers remaining down, slide the left thumb lightly up and down the side of the the neck.

Another exercise is the following: remove the thumb a bit from the neck. Place each finger on the D string, ascending and descending, in separate bows. Then play four quarter notes to a bow with the thumb removed. Do the same thing while applying the thumb lightly to the neck, the object being to memorize the sensation of a thumb that does not clutch the neck in order to support the violin.

Q. How high should the thumb come above the neck when playing?

A. I prefer a low thumb with a little bit of it above the fingerboard.

Q. How is a very long thumb placed?

A. More of the thumb will remain above the fingerboard.

Q. What about persons with short thumbs?

A. In that case it is natural for the thumb to contact the neck a bit lower. The important thing, however, is an upward pressure rather than a side pressure.

Q. How is the thumb placed in relation to the other fingers?

A. The thumb may be placed opposite the first finger, midway between the first and second fingers, or slightly behind the first finger (toward the scroll).

Q. Which is preferable?

A. Again that is a variable depending on the shape and size of the hand. When the left thumb is in a slightly backward position, it is more conducive to shifting to the higher positions with greater ease. For many players it is also more conducive to a more relaxed vibrato. However, many fine players who have a forward position of the thumb have marvelous left-hand techniques and beautiful vibratos.

Q. What sensation should the player feel in order to have correct action of the fingers of the left hand?

A. The player should feel that the action comes from the very base knuckles. Here is an exercise to help memorize that sensation.

Place a rubber band over the thumb and little finger on the back of the left hand. Both strands of the rubber band should be above the base knuckles toward the elbow. Try to bring the rubber band down to the finger tips by wiggling the fingers vigorously. This will be very difficult, but the finger action will be improved by just trying to succeed. Photo No. 1.

As we play the first, second, third, and fourth fingers on an ascending scale on any string, there should be a feeling of a rather precise and slightly energetic dropping of the finger.

Q. How much finger pressure should there be as the finger tip touches the string?

A. There should be only enough pressure to articulate the note clearly. Any additional finger pressure is of no value. It can be harmful to the finger tips only if the string is struck too violently. It also has a tendency to retard the velocity.

Q. What is the sensation when the finger is to be lifted from the string?

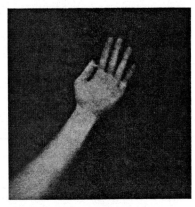

Photo No. 1

A. As an example let us consider a descending scale. The finger action, or the *sensation* of finger action, is a bit different from that of the ascending scale. It is that of producing a left hand pizzicato as the finger leaves the string. The finger must leave the string in a curved shape, which would be more or less sideways rather than upwards.

Some pupils with short arms will be greatly benefited if, when playing left-hand pizzicato, the elbow is inclined slightly toward the left of the violin or viola.

I would like to comment on the fact that when you place the fingers down, you find that you are doing what is quite natural. It might be related to the law of gravity. It is easier to place them down than to lift them up. More effort is required to lift the fingers from the string.

Q. How can I prepare the elementary pupil to "memorize the sensation" of achieving velocity as progress is made?

A. By teaching the pupil to place more than one finger down simultaneously particularly in descending passages.

Q. What exercises would you offer for this type of training?

A. On the elementary level I suggest placing the second finger down on the A string, note C natural, first position. (Ex. No. 1) With the second finger remaining down, place the fourth and third fingers down on the D string simultaneously. Learning to put two fingers down simultaneously is an efficient way to develop velocity and finger co-ordination.

We might go a step further and place the first finger down on the A string. (Ex. No. 2) Now try to place the fourth, third, and second fingers down on the D string simultaneously. It makes a very fine exercise. Do this a number of times.

A more difficult exercise, but one which is even more valuable, is the following: (Ex. No. 3) Place the second finger down on the A string, note C. Now place the fourth, third, and first fingers down on the D string simultaneously. Do this several times.

The same principle should be applied to descending scales. Place the first finger on the A string in the third position, note D. (Ex. No. 4) Shift downward to the note C, second finger in the first position. Instead of striking the second finger, try placing the first and second fingers down simultaneously (notes B and C).

Q. What suggestions do you have to develop excellent finger action?

A. To do this, one would have to play exercises that will include different types of finger activity. For example, normal finger action will take place when we play E natural and F natural one-half step apart on the D string. Here the fingers are squared to a certain extent. An example of this type of activity is found in Ex. No. 5.

The next type of finger activity occurs when the higher note is a whole step (a major second) higher. The higher finger is then in a slightly elongated position. (Ex. No. 6)

The third type of finger activity is the extension. Here the higher finger plays a minor third, which results in the widening of the web between the fingers. (Ex. No. 7)

The fourth type of finger activity is one which develops flexibility; (chromatic). The slide between one half step and another must be made with precision. (Ex. No. 8) More advanced pupils should try Ex. No. 9.

Ex. No. 1

silent study-without the bow

etc.

Ex. No. 2

without the bow

etc.

Ex. No. 3

without the bow

etc.

Ex. No. 4

With the bow

These exercises are to be practiced without music.
Repeat each measure at least 4 times.
Practice these in two ways: observing the slurs above the notes and then below.

Ex. No. 5

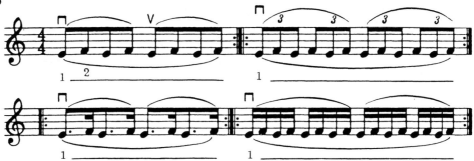

Ex. No. 6

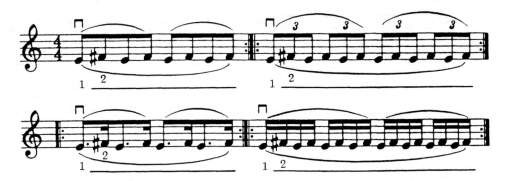

Ex. No. 7

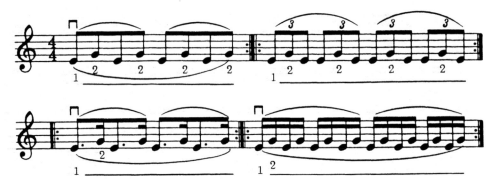

Ex. No. 8

Ex. No. 9

To be played two and four to a bow. Practice with both sets of fingerings. The bottom set is the conventional fingering and the top is the more modern set of fingering. With the top set of fingering, make sure that the thumb remains stationary and does not move with the finger change.

The fifth type of finger activity takes place when we go from one string to another. The finger should be lifted and placed on the next string. This should be done quickly, keeping the fingers as close to the string as possible. We might call this "horizontal action." The following exercise will serve as a basis for this type of practice. (Ex. No. 10)

Ex. No. 10

This exercise is purely a calisthenic for finger action and is not necessarily the best fingering for public performance.

Q. Should these exercises be applied to the higher positions?

A. By all means. They should be done in the second, third, fourth, fifth, sixth and seventh positions. In each position, of course, additional problems will present themselves.

Q. What are these additional problems?

A. The fingers of the left hand will have to apply greater pressure because the strings will be farther from the fingerboard. The bow weight will have to be greatly reduced. The bow contact will have to be gradually closer to the bridge.

Q. In the exercises nos. 5 through 8, do you want the lower fingers to remain down?

A. Yes, but they should also be practiced lifting both fingers. This should then be practiced in a slower tempo.

Q. In the very high positions, is it not sometimes impossible to play half-steps in tune if the lower finger remains down?

A. In order to make room for the higher finger, we must learn to lift the lower finger. The distances are then so small that we have to displace a finger to make the next higher finger low enough for good intonation.

Q. What do we expect from each finger from the standpoint of technical development?

A. We expect each finger to be able to:
1. play half-steps;
2. play whole steps;
3. play augmented seconds or minor thirds with adjacent fingers;
4. to develop flexibility by sliding from one note to another in half steps;
5. it also means developing that type of left-hand pizzicato action, leaving the string in a curved shape toward the base knuckle;
6. each finger must press on each string firmly enough to articulate the note and lightly enough to play harmonics (Ex. No. 11); there is a dual type of finger pressure which comes from the performance of artificial harmonics, where one finger is pressed firmly and the upper finger touches very lightly.

Q. How do we memorize the sensation of different finger pressures?

A. The following exercise will help you to memorize the sensation of different finger pressures. Place the third finger on the G string in the first position, note C. Press the finger firmly into the string. Now apply a little more of the finger pad to the string, and touch the string as lightly as possible. Do the same thing with the fourth finger. Do this on all strings. (Ex. No. 11)

Ex. No. 11

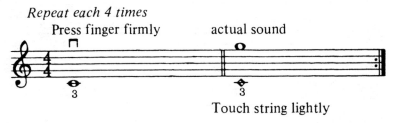

Ex. No. 12

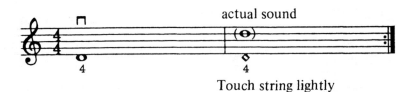

Each finger is also expected to play the so-called FLYING HARMONIC. Here the finger slides up to a harmonic and is lifted from the string when the harmonic sounds. On the up-bow, both the finger and the bow are lifted simultaneously. (Ex. No. 13)

Ex. No. 13

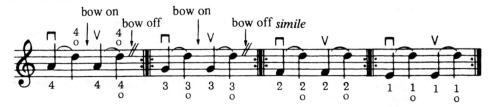

In the previous exercises, I have written out the various skills we expect from each finger. It would be a good idea to create exercises similar to these for the complete technical development of each finger.

A good calisthenic is to practice unisons in the following manner. They will help to develop a strong left hand and widen the web between the fingers. (Ex. No. 14)

Ex. No. 14

slowly

Q. How do we develop finger flexibility?

A. The following three exercises will be helpful in developing flexibility:

1. Place a rubber band around the four fingers of the left hand near the tips. Hold the left hand up as though playing the violin. Stretch the first finger as far away from the other three fingers as possible. Hold it there to the count of six. Do this four times. Photo No. 3.

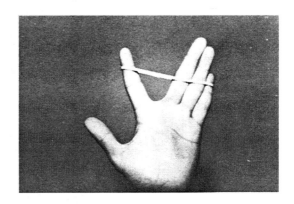

Photo No. 3

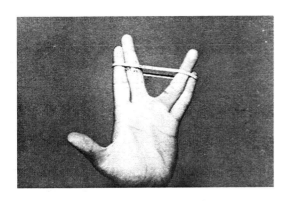

Photo No. 3A

Now move the first and second fingers away as far as possible from the third and fourth fingers. Hold this to the count of six. Photo No. 3A.

Now stretch the fourth finger, moving it away as far as possible from the first, second, and third fingers. Hold this to the count of six. Photo 3B.

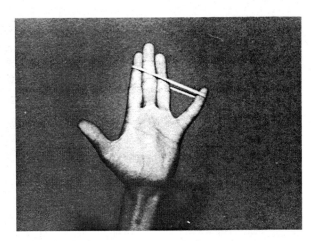

Photo No. 3B

Photo No. 3C

2. With the help of the thumb and first finger of the right hand, spread the first and second fingers of the left hand as far apart as possible. Hold the fingers apart to the count of six. Repeat this four times. Do the same with the other fingers. Photo 3C.

3. Place the three fingers down on the A string in a 2-3 pattern. (notes C# and D in the first position) Lift the first finger and place it on the D string (note E), but allow the second and third fingers to remain on the A string.

Slide the first finger from its regular position to as far back to the nut as possible. Do this sliding up and back eight times in slow quarter notes. You are now developing flexibility of the first finger. However, you must make sure that the second and third fingers remain firmly down on the A string. Try not to move your left thumb during this slide. (Ex. No. 15)

Ex. No. 15

Q. How do we develop velocity?

A. If we assume that the player has normally strong fingers, the ability to play quickly is to a great extent psychological. The player must learn to think and see ahead of the measure that is being played. One must be trained to see a whole passage ahead. This means developing a wider peripheral vision. Velocity means also a left hand that can perform clearly articulated trills.

Q. If velocity is dependent upon a good trill, how do we develop the trill?

A. A good trill is possible when we have a relaxed hand and when the fingers have been trained to snap back quickly with precision and speed.

Strong fingers per se, will not necessarily produce a good trill. A student can have strong fingers and yet lift them in a sluggish manner from the strings. Lifting the fingers from the string speedily will come when one practices exercises that include mordents. The mordent might well be the secret of a good trill because its performance encourages a snappy lifting of the finger from the string. The finger must always leave the string in a curved shape.

In the following exercise we learn to play scales using mordents. Combined with the martelé stroke, this type of exercise is conducive to developing a fine trill.

Lift the finger quickly from the string, accenting each quarter note. Leave a clean stop before starting the next note. Play scales in this manner. (Ex. No.16)

Ex. No. 16

Complete the scale

Advanced players should play two- and three-octave scales also in this manner.

Repeat each section of Ex. 17 four times without pausing using the entire bow. Gradually play faster and faster. When you play in a slow tempo, work the fingers very hard, lifting them rather high in a curved shape from the base joints. As you gradually increase the speed, keep the fingers closer to the strings and use less bow. (Ex. No. 17)

Ex. No. 17

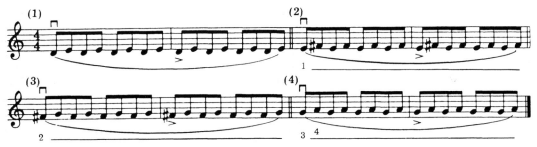

Q. Exactly how much finger weight must be applied to the strings as we play?

A. For normal playing, I like to feel that the weight of the finger supported by the base joint is sufficient. The object is to create a clear sound. The feeling must be that all finger action comes from the base joint, which is the source of the energy. For calisthenics, we might apply a little more effort to that finger. This does not necessarily mean "banging" the finger down on the string. That could be injurious.

We can make the finger work harder by playing slow passages, and as each finger falls on the string, press into the fingerboard as though it were made of rubber. This could be beneficial from the therapeutic standpoint. But that is not done when we play more rapidly. In the very high positions, a little more weight is required because the distance between the string and the fingerboard is greater.

Q. How do we strengthen the fingers of the left hand?

A. In principle we adopt the same approach as the athletes use to strengthen the muscles. Preparatory trill studies in each position will be very helpful. These trill studies are found in the book, **The Best of Sevcik, Vol. 1.** However, to make these exercises more effective, fill a small sack (about four inches long) with marbles or small stones. Using a short string, hang the sack from the scroll of the violin. The fingers will be strengthened by practicing trills and scales with the sack hanging from the scroll. Photo No. 4.

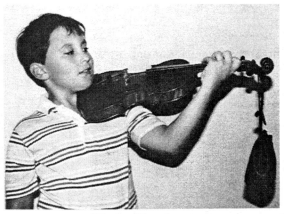

Photo No. 4

Playing scales with left-hand pizzicato in the first position will also strengthen the fingers of the left hand. (Ex. 18)

Ex. No. 18

Q. Are there any exercises to strengthen the left hand without using the violin?

A. Yes. Hold the left arm up as though playing the violin. Press the fingers into the palm of the hand as in Photo No. 5. Then bring the fingertips up so they press firmly into the base joints or knuckles of the fingers. Press to the count of six. Photo No. 6. Raise the first finger to its fullest extent, keeping all the other fingers down.

Photo No. 5

Photo No. 6

Do this eight times slowly. Do the same with each finger. After a few weeks alternate between two fingers: the first and second fingers, the second and third fingers, and the third and fourth fingers.

Another exercise to strengthen the fingers is the following: with the fingertips pressed into the base knuckles of each finger separate the first finger from the others in a lateral motion. Then take two fingers and by separating them from the others, move them to the right or to the left. Then do likewise with the little finger. Photos No. 7, 8, 9, and 10.

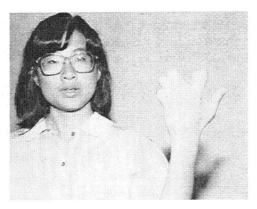

Photo No. 7

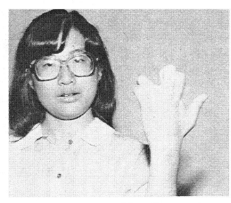

Photo No. 8

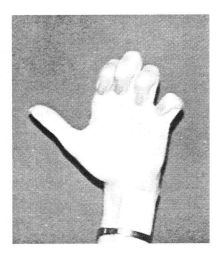

Photo No. 9

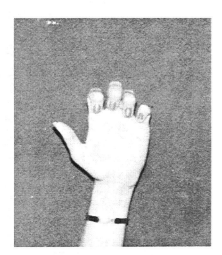

Photo No. 10

Then take the first and fourth fingers and move them away, leaving the tips of the two middle fingers down. As the fingers are apart hold them separated to the count of six.

Q. How do we develop finger independence?

A. Here are three silent specialized exercises that will help to develop finger independence:

1. Place your fingers in the Geminiani chord, one finger on each string. Press the first finger very firmly into the string while the other fingers remain on the strings touching very lightly. (Ex. No. 19) Photos No. 11 and 12.

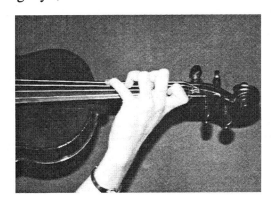

Photo No. 11

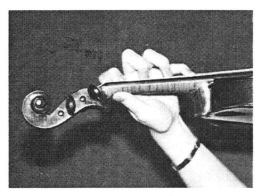

Photo No. 12

16

Concentrate on the firm pressure of the first finger to the count of ten. Try to imagine that the fingerboard is made of rubber and that the object is to sink the first finger into it. Press the second finger into the string and concentrate on firm pressure while the other fingers touch lightly. Do the same with the third and fourth fingers. The fingers that touch lightly should NOT LEAVE THE STRING.

Ex. No. 19

The Geminiani chord in two positions.
Practice the exercise in these two ways.

2. Place the fingers in the Geminiani chord. Raise and lower the first finger eight times in quarter notes, keeping the other fingers down FIRMLY on the string.

Do the same with the second, third, and fourth fingers, keeping the other fingers down. As time goes on, you may do this in eighth notes for as many beats as possible without tiring too much.

3. Place the fingers in the Geminiani chord. After you raise and lower each finger eight times, keeping the other fingers down, alternate between the first and second fingers, then between the second and third fingers, then the third and fourth fingers. Now alternate between the first and third fingers, then the second and fourth fingers. Do this in quarter notes, eighth notes, and sixteenth notes.

Now lift the first and second fingers simultaneously while the third and fourth fingers remain down. Do the same with the second and third fingers simultaneously. Likewise, do the same with the third and fourth fingers.

Q. Can you suggest another type of exercise that is not silent and that incorporates the use of the bow?

A. Yes. In the following exercise (Ex. No. 20) the fourth finger is kept down silently while the eighth notes are played.

Play each section four times. Start slowly. As you gain facility you may try to increase the speed.

Create similar exercises in the second, third, fourth, and fifth positions.

Ex. No. 20

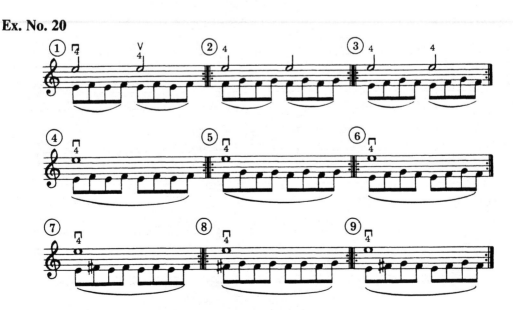

The Science of Scale Playing

Q. When do you start to teach scales?

A. Almost immediately. After a few lessons a pupil should be able to play a one-octave scale in D major. It only involves one finger pattern (the 2-3 pattern) on the D and A strings. The same finger pattern can be used on the G and D strings and on the A and E strings.

Q. What bowing instructions do you give for the very first time a pupil is to perform the scales?

A. They should be performed from the middle of the bow to a mark near the tip, using only the lower arm from the elbow joint. The opening and closing of the elbow is essential for this bowing.

Q. How do you decide where to put the mark near the tip?

A. You should help the student draw the bow as close to the tip as possible while the elbow still forms a slight obtuse angle. If the upper and lower arm form a straight line, or if the bow is not parallel to the bridge it means that the bow has been drawn too close to the tip. When playing at the tip, there should still be a slight obtuse angle between the upper and lower arm.

Q. Should the pupil start with half notes or quarter notes in the scales?

A. I start with quarter notes with a slight articulation between the notes. This bowing is called DETACHE LANCE.

Q. Should each note be played once or more than once?

A. It might be wise to play each note four times.

Q. Should the lower fingers be kept down?

A. Yes. That is essential until the shape of the left hand is well established.

Q. Do you recommend using the fourth finger in the scale or the open string?

A. In the beginning, I would suggest with some pupils, the use of the fourth finger be postponed for a short time as it may upset the shape of the left hand. The entire technic depends on how well the first finger is placed. That is why it is not always best to introduce all four fingers in the beginning unless the pupil starts off holding the violin in the guitar position. Then the fourth finger may be introduced almost immediately.

Q. How soon should various rhythms be introduced in the scales?

A. As soon as possible. The following examples will serve as guidelines and should be taught by rote. (Ex. No. 1)

Ex. No. 1

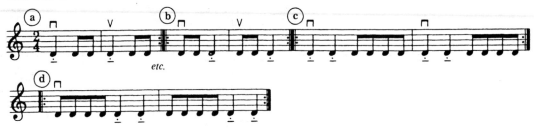

As a rule young children are very quick to learn various rhythms.

Q. How many different rhythms would you introduce during the same lesson?

A. The teachers will have to decide that.

Q. At what tempo should these scales be played?

A. I suggest a moderate working tempo, a quarter note to about M.M. 60 or a bit faster. In a heterogeneous string class where you play two-octave scales, the bass at a certain point will have to start lower. The same with the cello and viola. They should be coordinated so that a two-octave scale can be played in unison by all the strings.

Q. When should the minor scales be introduced?

A. I would say that minor scales should not be introduced until you feel that the pupils are ready for them. You want to impart a solid feeling of the major key before you introduce the minor.

Q. Do you teach all three minor scales?

A. Yes, but I would wait until the second year or so before teaching the harmonic minors.

Q. When do you introduce the two-octave scales?

A. The two-octave scales that may be introduced in the first position should be introduced early. The two-octave scales that go beyond the first position should be introduced as soon as the pupil can play in the third position and has started the fifth position.

Q. When do you introduce the three-octave scales?

A. When the pupil has started the seventh position. We begin by teaching the major keys of G, A, A flat, and B flat.

Q. How do you start teaching the seventh position?

A. You must first learn how to find the first finger on each string in the seventh position. It will sound an octave higher than the open string. Then find the proper placement for the second, third, and fourth fingers on each string. The left thumb is to be placed approximately at right angles to the fingerboard. Do this by rote.

Q. What materials do you use for teaching the seventh position?

A. The Best of Sevcik, Book 1, followed by **Sitt, Op. 32, Book 4**, which has studies in the sixth and seventh positions as well as studies that shift from the first to the sixth and seventh positions.

Q. The quality of sound in the seventh position poses a problem. What suggestions have you for developing a beautiful tone in the high positions?

A. What you should keep in mind is that the left hand finger pressure becomes firmer and that the bow weight on the string becomes less. When you play in the higher positions the fingers play forte and the bow plays piano. The bow must also be drawn closer to the bridge.

Q. Do you suggest playing on the fingertips or more on the pads of the fingers in the higher positions?

A. That is determined mostly by the shape of the player's hand and whether the vibrato is used. The vibrato may make it necessary to use more of the pad of the finger.

Q. What is a good basic set of fingerings to start the three-octave scales?

A. If you adopt the format that is found in the last six pages of the **Hrimaly Scale Book** you will find the following fingerings very practical. They are referred to as the "Paganini-Flesch fingerings."

Each scale is to start with the second finger on the G string. You then play a half step below the tonic with the first finger before ascending the three octaves. The highest tonic is always repeated before descending.

Here we have a C major scale in three octaves, using the Paganini-Flesch fingering.

Ex No. 2

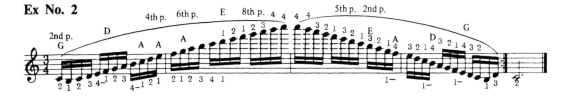

On the ascending scales try to keep the fourth finger down for an instant while you play the first finger on the next higher string. The principle of keeping one finger down also applies as you descend.

You might refer to this as the "Anchor Principle." It means that one finger is kept down on one string while another finger is being placed on another string. It gives you the feeling of solidity in that position, and is worthwhile developing even though it takes time and patience.

Here is the fingering formula as it is presented in numbers. It should be memorized.

C Major Scale

C major scale

	shift on A	shift on E	descend	shift			
G string	D	A ↓	E str.↓		descend	A str.	D str.	G str.

‖: 2 1 2 3 4 | 1 2 3 4 | 1 2 1 2 1 2 | 3 4 1 2 | 1 2 3 4 | 4 4 4 3 2 | 1 3 2 1 3 2 1 | 4 3 2 1 | 4 3 2 1 | 4 3 2 1 3 | 2 :‖
4—   4—   1   restez   1—   1—   1—

After you have memorized this fingering it will be quite easy to play the following major scales by rote, using the same fingerings as in the above C major scale. They all start with the second finger on the G string.

D flat D	starting in the third position
E flat E	starting in the fourth position
F F sharp	starting in the fifth position
G flat	starting in the sixth position

Notice that the numbers refer to fingerings on that particular string. For the major scales you descend on the E string - 44321-321, etc.

The fingerings for the following major scales are slightly different. They should be memorized.

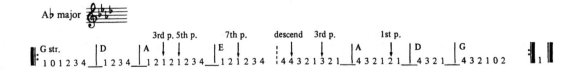

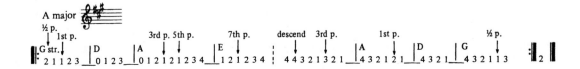

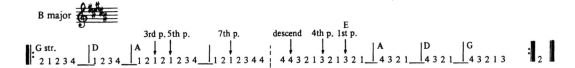

Q. Is there a similar type of fingering formula for the melodic minor scales?

A. Yes. Here is the C melodic minor scale in three octaves, using the Paganini-Flesch fingerings. As in the major scales, you start with the 2nd finger on the G string. In all the minor scales you descend 432-321 etc., and NOT 44321 as in the major scales. (Ex. No. 3)

Ex. No. 3

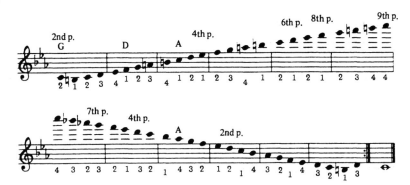

After you have memorized this fingering formula for the C minor scale you will be able to play the following minor scales using this same formula. They all start with the second finger on the G string.

C sharp minor - starting in the second position

D minor   - starting in the third position

D sharp minor - starting in the third position

E flat minor   - starting in the fourth position

F minor   - starting in the fifth position

F sharp minor - starting in the fifth position

The fingerings for the following minor scales are slightly different. They should be memorized.

Ex. No. 4

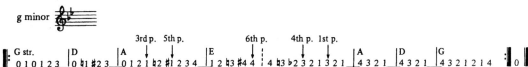

22

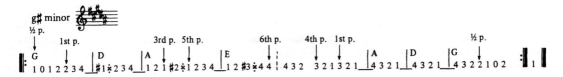

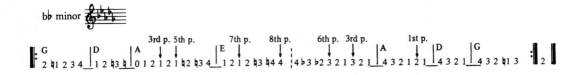

Here are the three-octave major and minor scales using the Paganini-Flesch fingerings based on the Hrimaly settings.

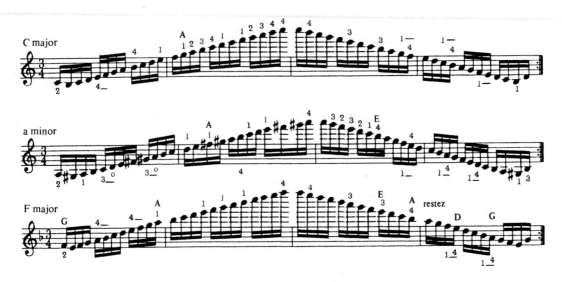

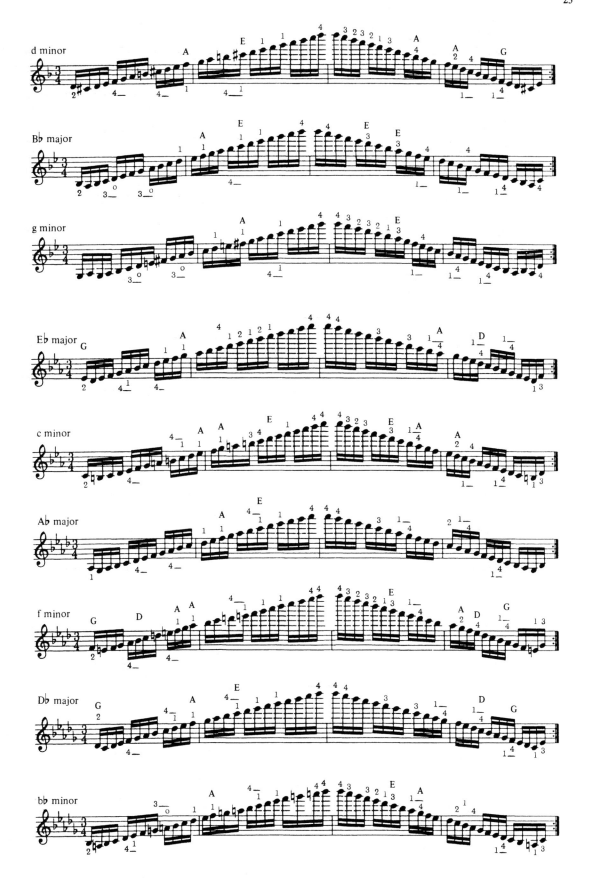

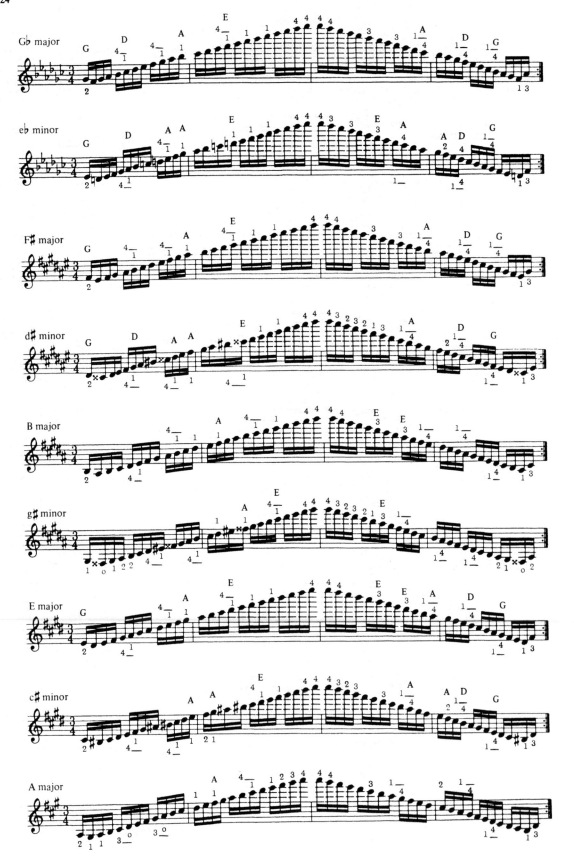

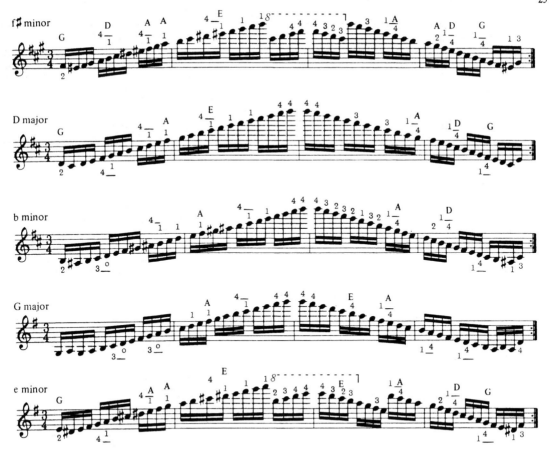

Q. How long shall we continue to play the three-octave scales with these fingerings?

A. That is up to the teacher, who will be guided by the ability of the pupil. The Paganini-Flesch fingerings is a good basic formula. However, there are others.

When a pupil has reasonably well mastered one set, an alternative formula should be introduced. You should tell your students that there is always more than one way to finger a passage.

Q. What are the basic requirements for a good performance of any scale?

A. They are:
1. a beautiful tone, a cognizance of the different lanes in relation to the pitch and bow weight. The higher the pitch the closer the bow is drawn to the bridge;
2. smooth string change;
3. intonation, checking notes as frequently as possible;
4. clean and accurate shifting;
5. playing the scales in different speeds and dynamics;
6. playing the scales that involve various bowing projects.

Q. In what order would you introduce the various bowing projects?

A. Here is a suggested order:

THE DETACHÉ PROJECT (use the following):
1. the whole bow;
2. the upper ½ (U ½) and the lower ½ (L ½);
3. the upper ⅓ (U ⅓) and the lower ⅓ (8 inches of bow);
4. U ¼ (U ¼) and the L ¼ (6 inches of bow);
5. U ⅙ and the L ⅙ (4 inches of bow);
6. U ¹⁄₁₂ and the L ¹⁄₁₂ (2 inches of bow, concentrating on the hand and fingers);
7. practice these bowing in different speeds.

THE MARTELÉ PROJECT

Practice the MARTELÉ in the same parts of the bow as suggested in the DETACHÉ project.

THE COLLÉ PROJECT

Play each scale all down-bows, all up-bows, then alternate down and up-bows in the following places on the bow:

1. at the frog;
2. six inches from the frog;
3. in the middle;
4. six inches from the tip;
5. at the tips.

The bow hair must be well set into the string before starting each note. At the middle and above, the tempo must be much slower.

THE SPICCATO PROJECT

Play each scale using the spiccato bowing in three places on the bow:

1. at the frog;
2. about six inches from the frog;
3. around the middle of the bow.

THE SAUTILLÉ PROJECT

Play each scale bouncing each note:

1. four times;
2. two times;
3. then three times.

THE STACCATO PROJECT

1. Slur the first notes of the scale in a down-bow. Play the rest of the ascending three-octave scale, using the staccato stroke in a single up-bow. Do this in eighth notes. In descending, slur the first two notes legato, and then play the rest of the scale using the staccato stroke in a single bow;

2. Play the first three notes as a legato triplet and complete the scale in triplet rhythm using the staccato stroke in a single up-bow. Descending, slur the first three notes, and continue as in #1. Do the same slurring the first four notes;

3. Play the first six notes smoothly in one bow as a sextolet. Continue the scale in that rhythm using the staccato stroke. Descending, slur the first six notes and continue with the staccato bowing;

4. Play the first eight notes smoothly in one bow and continue as in the above exercises. Each new rhythmic group should comprise a single beat in order to gradually develop velocity.

THE RICOCHÉT PROJECT

Play each scale in the following ways:

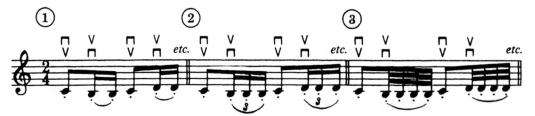

Q. In addition to the different styles of bowings, what rhythms would you suggest that we use for the scales to be played legato?

A. Here are a few of the many rhythms that may be used:

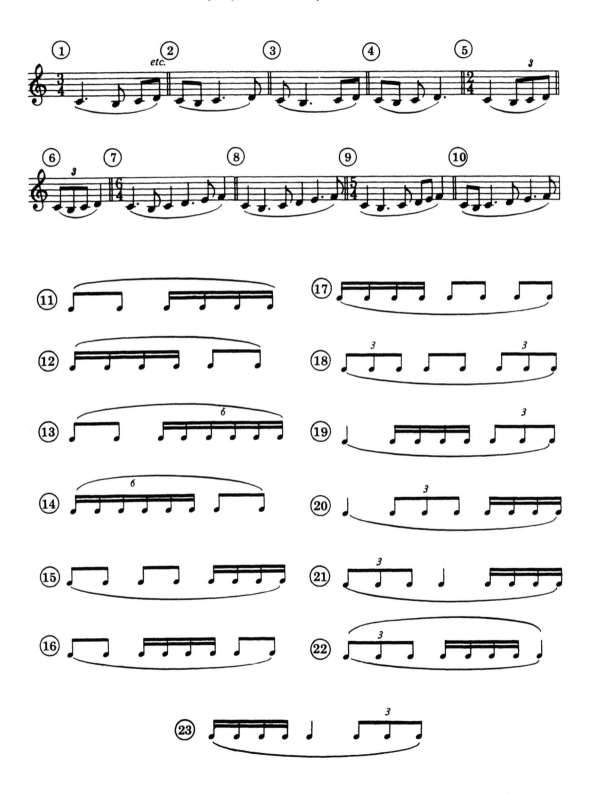

28

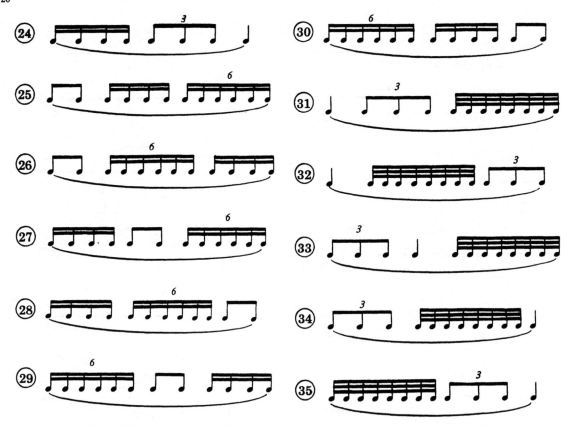

The above rhythms are to be applied to the Hrimaly setting of the three-octave scales.

Here we have mixed bowings. The separated notes should be practiced in 2 ways, using the detaché bowing and then the martelé bowing. F.M.T. means that the variation is to be practiced at the frog, middle and tip, using about 2 inches of bow with the hand and fingers.

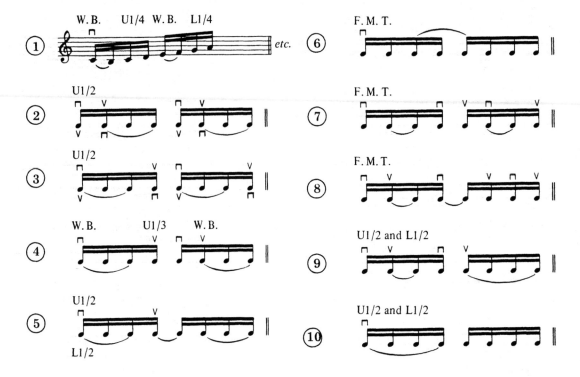

U1/2 and L1/2

(11)

W. B.

(12)

W. B.

(13)

p f p f p f p f p f p f

Start at the frog - gradually get to the tip and back - use 2 inches of bow.

(14)

Q. How important are scales in broken thirds?

A. They are valuable in developing smooth string changes as well as the skill of keeping one finger down while the finger on the next string is being placed. Broken fourths are also extremely valuable.

Q. How soon do you introduce the four-octave scales?

A. Only when the pupil can play the three-octave scales very well and has developed enough thumb technic to get around the fingerboard reasonably well.

Here are the four-octave scales in a numerical formula. Notice the following: the scales that start with open G, B, or B flat ascend on the E string from the third to the sixth position.

The scales that start on A flat and A ascend on the E string from the third to the fifth position.

From the highest octave all the scales descend with 4, 3, 2, 1. Do not repeat the top tonic as you descend.

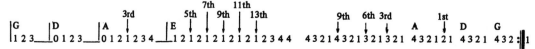

Bb major

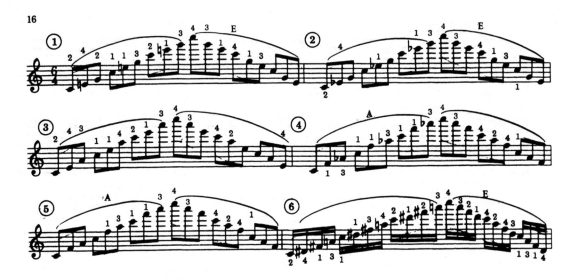

bb minor - B major - b minor

Q. How do you teach the arpeggios?

A. In the various chords. Here is an example of the arpeggios that are to be used with the C major scale. This should be done in conjunction with the scales in all the keys.

Q. How do you suggest that the arpeggios be practiced?

A. Slowly; then gradually more rapid. Isolate the various shifts and practice each one many times. Here is a pattern that should be used for each key. In many respects arpeggios are even more important than the scales in developing a fluent technic.

Q. How can a student develop a smooth connection when going from one string to another.

A. A good legato can be achieved in the following ways: As you play, allow the bow hair to gradually approach the next string following the curvature of the bridge. This may be described as a vertical curve. This string change should not be accented. To ensure a perfect legato the last finger on one string must remain down until the first finger on the next string is placed. This principle is also applied to arpeggios. Use the left hand as a pianist pedals when going from one note to another. This is the "Anchor Principle."

Q. Is it desirable for a player to learn to place several fingers on a string simultaneously?

A. Yes. When going from one string to another and when making a descending shift. The following exercise will help to develop left-hand efficiency:

Play each exercise several times. Lift all the fingers before repeating. Only the top note will be played or sounded.

These exercises are to be practiced without music. They are difficult, but just attempting to play them is very valuable.

Q. When do you introduce chromatic scales?

A. A chromatic scale in the first position may be introduced during the first or second year of study at the discretion of the teacher. It is a necessary aid to good intonation as it encourages careful listening.

Students are likely to underestimate the distance between the half steps, particularly in the first position.

Q. What fingerings do you use for the chromatic scales?

A. Here are two sets of fingerings. They should be practiced two and four notes to a bow.

Practice with both sets of fingerings. The bottom set is the conventional fingering and the top is the more modern set of fingering. With the top fingering, make sure that the thumb remains stationary and does not move with the finger change.

The Study of the Positions

The Art and Science of Shifting

Q. How long should a pupil remain in the first position?

A. That is difficult to answer because we are not all alike as far as aptitude for the instrument is concerned. I would say that the average student of age 8 or 9 should remain in the first position about six months — perhaps a bit less or longer. From the technical standpoint, we do not start the positions until the intonation is reasonably well established in the first position.

There was a time when many teachers would say that the student would have to stay in the first position for at least twelve to eighteen months. I disagree with that. Some pupils can start the third position as early as the sixth month. In a class situation, however, it would be at the discretion of the teacher.

Q. What position would you teach immediately after the first position?

A. I would suggest proceeding to the third position.

Q. Why not the second position?

A. It is purely a question of security. In the third position the base of the palm of the hand has a way of contacting the right rib of the instrument that seems to offer additional security.

Q. Why don't we start with the third position instead of the first position at the very beginning of violin study?

A. That is a very good question. As a matter of fact there are a number of teachers who do start with the third position, but this approach has not gained wide popularity. If good results are obtained by starting in the third position, the teacher should continue with this method. If we can judge by the number of teachers who start with the first position, I would say that that is probably more successful. Two possible objections to starting violin study in the third position may be the loss of the open string and increased difficulty of playing scales.

Q. How would you introduce the third position?

A. I would tell the student the following:
1. place the third finger on the D string, first position, note G;
2. sing the note;
3. place the first finger on the D string where the neck meets the rib of the violin. (approx. fifth position);
4. allow the thumb to be slightly under the neck and the palm to lightly contact the right rib of the instrument;
5. slowly slide the first finger back to the note G, which is in the third position;
6. allow the tip of the thumb to slightly face the scroll so that the thumb forms an acute angle to the neck.

Q. Why slide from the fifth position to third position rather than from first to third?

A. It is more conducive to achieving an ideal shape of the hand in the third position.

Q. Do you use printed music when you introduce the third position?

A. No. All new skills should be introduced by rote. When the pupil can find the first finger in the third position it must be checked with the next lower string in the manner below. That is the reason I suggest starting on the D string. You have a lower string with which to check the intonation.

We then do this on all strings!

Q. After the pupil can find the first finger in the third position, what is the next step?

A. The next step is to introduce the second finger on each string, testing each note in the following manner:

At the next lesson you may introduce the third and fourth fingers on each string. On the G and D strings, the third and fourth fingers are a half step apart. On the A and E strings, the second and third fingers are a half step apart.

At this point you should practice finger patterns on each string in various tempos and bowings. They should be learned by rote.

Practice this also on the D string.

Practice this also on the E string.

The next skill to develop without music is the ability to go smoothly from one string to another in the third position. Actually, this skill should be developed in all positions by the use of the "anchor setting" of the fingers.

A two-octave scale in the third position played without music should follow. It is to be played in various bowings and rhythms.

Q. May we then start reading music in the third position?

A. Yes. There are several good string methods available which will provide an interesting and effective way to learn the third position.

Q. How will you teach shifting for the first time?

A. We will start with the simplest shift, and that is where you go from one position to another with the same finger. In this shift, as in all the others, you must hear the note in your mind before you play it. You lighten the finger and thumb pressure during the slide. You must also bring the bow a bit closer to the bridge when you shift to a higher position. As the shift is made, the thumb must gradually pass under the neck, particularly when you ascend to the third position and above. During the shift it might be advisable to allow a very slight additional head pressure, and to hold the violin a bit higher than the shoulder.

Q. Do you also suggest developing each type of shift without printed music?

A. Yes, in order to memorize the sensation of the distance and to develop a kinesthetic sense of the fingerboard. Practice each shift without the bow, then with the bow.

Here is a way to learn the simple shift, going from one position to another with the same finger. Below, "t" means to test the note with the open string.

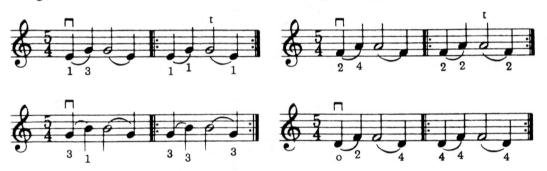

Do these exercises on all strings.

Q. How do we perform an ascending shift when we go from one finger to a higher finger?

A. If the two notes are slurred, you ascend or shift with the finger that is already on the string. That finger slides approximately to the position you are going to. When you arrive at the approximate position, the finger you are going to then drops down on to the string. If this shift occurs in a singing passage, lift the lower finger as soon as you reach the note you are going to play. You will then vibrate with much greater ease.

Q. If the two notes occur when there is no slur, what is the rule?

A. When the two notes are not in a slur, you shift to the higher note with the finger that you are going to, and not with the finger that is already on the string. This, of course, means that the two notes are in separate bows.

Q. How do you shift from one position to another with different fingers when they are only one step or a half step apart?

A. We might refer to this as the diatonic shift or the scale line shift. This is the shift that is used in scale passages. You always shift with the finger that you are going to, whether the notes are *slurred* or in *separate bows*. Actually, the lower finger displaces the upper finger.

You are actually shifting from a higher finger to a lower finger, even though the lower finger goes to a higher pitch.

Q. What is the rule in the descending shifts, or when we go from a higher position to a lower position?

A. The rule is that you always shift with the finger that is on the string, whether the notes are slurred or in separate bows. The rule holds true in all the various types of shifts, including the scale line shift. In other words, we always shift with the finger that is on the string when we descend.

The following is a summary of the BASIC RULES OF SHIFTING:
1. when we shift from one position to another with different fingers IN A SLUR, we shift with the finger that is *already on the string*, whether ascending or descending;
2. we ascend with the finger that we are going to, and *not with the finger that is already on the string;*
   (a) when there is no slur (separate bows) and
   (b) when we shift from a higher finger to a lower finger;
3. when descending, we always shift with the finger that is already on the string.

However, and this is important, we may break the above rules whenever we wish to do so for musical reasons.

Q. How do we shift when two strings are involved or when we cross strings?

A. The rules are the same. If the two notes are in a slur, we slide with the finger that is on the string to the approximate position of the higher note, and then the higher finger drops onto the other string. If they are in separate bows, most of the shift is done with the finger that we are going to. Here a subtle bow action is required depending upon the emotional content of the work and how much of the shift to the higher note you wish to be heard.

The following examples describe two different ways. The small notes indicate the fingers that do the shifting. They are not to be sounded.

Q. Is there a way to go from one position to an adjacent position without shifting?

A. Yes. I would not call this an actual shift. I would say that we stretch to another position. The technic of stretching a minor third of fourth should be cultivated and used more frequently. It is a precise way to go to another position where the change is not to be heard because there is no auxiliary note.

If after you have stretched to the next position and you wish to remain in that position, you then allow the hand to follow.

Another way of saying this is: in any given position we should be able to stretch to the next higher position with just the finger while the hand remains in the original position. If, however, you wish to remain in the new position, the hand should follow. You should also be able to reach back to a lower position while your hand remains in the original position.

Q. What are some of the important principles to bear in mind in order to develop a good left thumb technic?

A. When shifting from the first to the third position, I do not suggest that the thumb go forward in advance of the fingers. I would like to see a very slight movement of the lower part of the hand in advance of the fingers. It gives you the feeling of unlocking the hand in preparation for the shift.

Q. How does the thumb technic apply as you descend from the third to the first position?

A. In descending, it is advisable for the thumb to slightly precede the hand, or to move simultaneously with the hand.

Q. How does the thumb move when going from the third to the fifth position?

A. When you shift from the third to the fifth position, the thumb must act swiftly and get around and under so that it is practically at right angles to the neck of the violin.

Q. Where does the thumb contact the neck?

A. The joint in the middle of the thumb might lie directly under the center of the neck. However, the size of the thumb will often determine exactly where that contact takes place.

From the fifth to the higher positions less of the thumb remains on the neck, depending on the size of the thumb and the hand.

When you descend from the high positions, you must bear in mind that the thumb actually takes the initiative.

Q. Does the thumb continue to move around in the very high positions?

A. Actually not. With many hands, when the player reaches the seventh position and above, the thumb can remain stationary. Some players may have to bring it around a bit more. This all depends on the size of the hand.

Q. But suppose you are playing in the twelfth or thirteenth position and the hand is too small to allow the thumb to remain on the neck?

A. In that case it is permissible for the thumb to leave the neck and to be placed on the rib. Many players allow the thumb to slide on the side of the fingerboard.

Q. How about the elbow during the shift?

A. The elbow travels slightly to the right. The moving of the thumb around and under the neck and the moving of the elbow a bit to the right must be carefully coordinated.

Q. How would you summarize the placement of the thumb in the various positions?

A. In the following ways:
1. In the 2nd position the thumb is placed exactly as it is in the first position, lying opposite the first finger or slightly behind it. However, this is a variable.
2. In the 3rd position the thumb might be placed a bit under the neck and the hand a bit to the right of the neck.
3. In the 4th position the flat part of the thumb rests on the curve in the beginning of the neck. The first joint lies slightly to the left of the center of the neck.
4. In the 5th position the thumb is practically at right angles to the neck. The joint lies directly under the center of the neck.

Photo No.13

5. In the higher positions less of the thumb remains on the neck, all depending upon the size of the hand.
6. In shifting upward from the first position to a higher position, the thumb does not act independently, but moves upward with the hand.
   To ensure great freedom of the hand in shifting:
   a. Make sure that the thumb does not cling too firmly to the neck of the instrument.
   b. Make sure that the violin is held a bit more firmly under the jaw at the very moment that the shift is made.

Photo No. 14

7. In shifting downward from a higher position, the thumb invariably precedes the hand, and after the thumb has reached backward, it must pull the hand after it.

8. In ascending, the thumb moves upward with the hand, but in descending, the thumb may move first with the hand following.

Q. Have you any guidelines that will tell us how quickly shifts are to be performed?

A. Yes. The speed of the shift comes under two categories. The first is the transitional shift which should not be heard. It should be performed as cleanly as possible. You might think of the pianists. We do not hear any intermediate notes when they decend, or ascend, or when they go from one octave to another.

A transitional shift has no emotional significance. It is purely a mechanical convenience in order to get from one position to another. Frequently it will involve a principle of extension and contraction of the hand in order to have the finger ready in advance for the note to which the shift is to be made.

In the following example, where I have the letter "a", straighten and extend the fourth finger while you play the second finger (G#) marked with the arrow (↑). The fourth finger will now be ready in advance to shift to the next note (4th finger, G#) marked with the arrow (↑).

At letter "b" you are to contract the fingers, particularly the fourth finger, so that it will become closer to the note G# in the third position. While you are playing the G# with the second finger (marked ↓) the fourth finger is contracted so that it will be brought closer to the next note G# (↓) in the third position.

4th finger is extended.　　　4th finger is contracted.

Q. What is the second type of shift?

A. The second type or shift is called the "expressive shift." Here the speed of the shift is determined by musical taste and the emotional content of the work.

I would like to suggest that you listen carefully to each shift, and to play it with various speeds and finger pressures.

You must be motivated to make definite decisions on how much of the shift you wish to hear. The emotional content of the work may warrant an expressive shift that should be heard.

Lighten the finger pressure on the string during the slide. If it is a long shift, the bow pressure should also be lessened.

Q. When is it permitted to allow the thumb to come more under the neck?

A. When playing difficult four-part chords, the wrist or the hand should move inward toward the neck.

You permit the thumb to come more under the neck when you prepare to ascend into a higher position. I chose a harmonic so as to lighten the finger pressure on the string for the higher note. The left thumb must not press the side of the neck too firmly and the fourth finger must move lightly.

Q. When do you introduce the development of the thumb technic in the higher positions?

A. I like to present thumb technic toward the end of the second year of instruction. With talented children, it can be introduced after a few months of study, with even less time for the very gifted child.

Q. How would you begin?

A. With a one-octave scale with the first finger on one string.

Below, "t" means to test note with the open string.

Q. How do we introduce thumb technic with the use of the other fingers?

A. With one-octave scales on one string with one finger at a time.

Q. Would you continue these with alternate fingerings?

A. By all means.

You must also strengthen the sensation of the thumb moving with the hand and gradually passing under the neck when going to the fourth position and above.

Q. How would you accomplish this?

A. First, without the bow. Place one finger on each string in the Geminiani chord.

With the fingers remaining on the string, slide the hand up to approximately the seventh position several times. During the slide keep the fingers about the same distance apart. When the hand is in the seventh position, the thumb should contact the base of the neck midway between the tip of the thumb and the first joint. There is a slight sensation of pushing the hand in ascending and of pulling in descending.

Q. How do you introduce harmonics?

A. I introduce harmonics with the fourth finger in the third position by telling the student the following:

1. place the fingers down on the A string in the third position;
2. hold the fourth finger for two beats;
3. remove the three lower fingers;
4. without moving the hand, flatten out the fourth finger and slide it a full step above the regular fourth-finger note.

In most cases the pupil will be able to find that harmonic without any trouble. The difficulty will come when the pupil is asked to hold the finger lightly on the string. Pupils are likely to press the fourth finger down to the fingerboard. We ask the pupil to just let the fourth finger lightly touch the string without pressing down at all. The pupil should look at the finger as it is placed on the string.

Q. What is the difference in bow pressure when playing the four notes in the third position leading to the harmonic and the bow pressure when playing the harmonic?

A. There is a very subtle difference, and we have to experiment. The harmonic can actually have as much bow pressure as the solid note.

Q. What lane do you use when playing harmonics?

A. In a slightly higher lane, closer to the bridge.

Q. Is it possible to use different styles of bowings when playing harmonics?

A. Yes.

Q. What exercises would you recommend to continue the study of harmonics?

A. I recommend the following exercises as a systematic way of studying harmonics:

Ex. No. 13

Ex. No. 14

Q. Many professional players remove the finger from the harmonic while the note continues to sound. How would you teach that technic?

A. That is a very valuable technic. I call it the "Flying Harmonic." It should be practiced in the following manner:

1. play a harmonic note for two beats on the D string;
2. remove the finger suddenly and quickly;
3. at the same time adjust the speed and weight of the bow to encourage the harmonic to sound after the finger has been removed from the string.

Q. Does the bow weight and speed really change when the finger is lifted from the harmonic note?

A. Yes. It does change. The degree of change must be determined by the player. If it is on a lower string, the change would be slightly different than if it were on a higher string. If it were on a higher string, the speed may have to slacken a bit. If it were on a lower string, the speed may have to be greater. Bow pressure on the string would have to be altered. The player must experiment and determine what works best for the instrument.

Q. Would the lane also have to be changed?

A. Slightly. I am sure that better results can be obtained by moving the bow closer to the bridge when playing a harmonic.

Q. What various bowings would you use when teaching harmonics?

A. The first one would be long sustained tones. Then I would introduce the détaché in eighth notes, then spiccato, then sautillé.

Q. Would you suggest that a student use harmonics to tune the instrument?

A. Yes, particularly the cello and bass.

Q. When do you introduce the remaining natural harmonics?

A. Almost immediately. A very good exercise to teach harmonics and to develop a kinesthetic sense of the fingerboard is to ask the pupil to find every natural harmonic on the entire string. Each harmonic should be held for four counts.

Be sure that when playing above the fourth position that the left thumb is placed well under or to the right of the fingerboard, parallel to the neck.

As the higher harmonics are played, the thumb goes under the fingerboard so that only the tip of the thumb is in contact with the base of the neck.

How to Develop Good Intonation

Q. What suggestions can you offer to develop good intonation?

A. The notes to be played must first be heard in the mind. Singing or humming the notes is very helpful. Students should be taught to sing the various intervals. The study of intervals can be made very interesting.

For example, play a whole note on the open D string. Ask the student to sing a major second or third, etc. above that note.

Q. What about the physical problems of good intonation?

A. Pupils should be asked to memorize the sensation of the hand in a normal position, which is the interval of a fourth between the first finger and the fourth finger. A good idea is to have the pupil place the first finger and the fourth finger on the D string. Then, leaving the first finger on the D string, place the fourth finger on the A string. This is an octave, and it represents the frame of the "normal" left-hand position.

Q. Isn't there a slight difference in the sensation when the fourth finger is placed on the same string and when it is placed on the next higher string?

A. Yes. There are subtle differences in the sensations. There is a slight additional stretch from the first to the fourth because of the slight widening of the web between the fingers. However, the important thing is that the pupil memorizes the sensation of the interval of the fourth.

Q. When the pupil leaves the frame, don't we have another problem?

A. Yes. When the first finger is lowered to a half-step from the nut, and the fourth finger is played, a slightly unnatural position results.

Q. What happens to the thumb when the first finger is lowered?

A. The thumb and the hand must remain in the same position. The pupil must develop the skill of bringing the first finger back without upsetting the frame or in any way altering the shape of the hand. That may be a difficult sensation for some pupils to memorize.

Q. Is there any exercise that you can suggest even before we do this on the instrument?

A. Here is one. Hold the hand up without the violin or viola as though playing. With the second, third and fourth fingers remaining quiet, stretch the first finger back from the base knuckle. Hold it there to the count of four. Now bring the first finger foreword to the normal position. Reach back and forth in quarter notes a number of times.

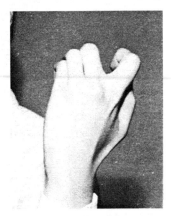

Photo No. 15

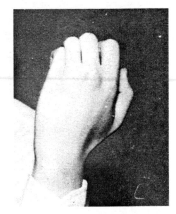

Photo No. 16

When your pupils memorize the sensation of bringing the first finger back without moving the other fingers, they will find it easier to leave the frame without disturbing the shape of the hand. On the instrument the pupils must hear the sound of the flatted first finger. But before they can hear it, they must memorize the physical sensation of bringing the first finger back and widening the web between the first and second fingers.

Q. Why is it that beginners frequently play out of tune with the second, third, and fourth fingers as soon as the first finger is brought back close to the nut?

A. The web between the first and second fingers is widened. It will be helpful if the pupils memorize the sensation of stretching the third and fourth fingers just a bit higher.

Of course, the distances between the second, third, and fourth fingers are not greater; they merely feel a bit greater.

The next skill to develop is a kinesthetic sense of the fingerboard. Long shifts should be practiced very slowly, both ascending and descending. The following must be memorized:
1. the distances between the notes,
2. just how far the thumb and the arm must be brought under the neck,
3. how soon the palm of the hand is to touch the body of the instrument.

Q. What about the visual aspect of good intonation

A. That is important. You must look at the fingerboard when practicing slowly to learn just where the note is to be found and to determine how far that note is from the end of the fingerboard. Pretend that there is an indentation on the fingerboard at the exact spot where the note is to be found. Measure in your mind:
1. the distance of the shift;
2. the remaining distance to the end of the fingerboard.

You might also measure the distance from that spot to where the neck joins the body of the instrument.

Q. What intervals are most likely to be played out of tune?

A. From my experience I believe that the notes most likely to be played out of tune are the third degree of the minor scale and the seventh degree of the major and minor scales. In minor I like the third degree of the scale a bit lower than when played on a piano, and the seventh degree a bit higher.

The next are the augmented seconds between the sixth and the seventh degrees of the harmonic minor scale. I like the sixth a bit lower and the seventh a bit higher. But at all times we must listen carefully to the diminished fifths and the diminished sevenths.

Some players are apt to be too permissive about notes that are slightly out of tune. This applies to both teacher and student.

It is possible to divide teachers into two categories:
1. those who are conscientious about virtuosity at the expense of good intonation;
2. those who are meticulous about intonation at the expense of the emotional content of the music.

There are many intervals which young players are likely to play out of tune, and these are usually half-steps. An example of this may be found in the chromatic scales. When playing F natural on the D string with the second finger in the first position, there is a tendency to play the F sharp a bit too low.

Q. What intervals are likely to be played out of tune in the higher positions?

A. In the three- and four-octave scales ascending, there is a tendency in the high positions to play notes too high. In descending, there is a tendency to play some notes too low. In the high positions we must remember that a half-step is so close that frequently the lower finger must be moved to make room for the next higher finger.

Q. About what position would that start?

A. That would depend on the width of the player's fingers, but it can certainly start from the sixth position.

The value of comparing as many notes as possible to the open strings is very obvious, and should become part of the pupil's training from the very start.

The real challenge is to adjust the intonation so that the listener does not detect the change. You must learn to practice many passages with and without the vibrato. When you practice without the vibrato, play very slowly.

Q. Are there different types of intonation?

A. Yes.

Q. What are the different types of intonation?

A. There are two types of intonation:
1. "tempered", and
2. "just", which is also called "natural" and sometimes "expressive" intonation.

Q. What is "tempered" intonation?

A. That is the distribution of imperfections among the intervals within the octave so that the semi-tones are made more or less equal. This is the way a piano is tuned. When playing with a piano the fifths and the minor thirds and sixths are a bit less than the true or mathematically correct intervals; the thirds, fourths, sixths, and minor sevenths are a bit larger.

Q. What is "natural" intonation?

A. "Natural" intonation uses the mathematically correct or true scale. It is also referred to as "expressive" intonation. When using "expressive" intonation we realize that the twelve intervals in a chromatic scale are not equally distant. In every chromatic scale the chromatic half-steps (e.g. F to F sharp) are larger than the diatonic half-steps (e.g. F to G flat).

When a string player plays with a pianist, the intonation is adjusted to the piano; there is no choice. But when playing with a group of strings, each player tempers the notes slightly to achieve good intonation.

Q. You speak frequently about fundamental tones. Will you comment on that?

A. If you wish to make a profound study of intonation, you must train yourself to listen to these fundamental tones. If you play double-stops, you will hear certain undertones which are one or two octaves lower. It is a good way to test your intonation and deepen your listening skills.

Play a double-stop in forte, using whole bows and holding each note four to eight beats. A low fundamental tone will be heard, but only by the player. This will take some practice.

In the following example the diamond shaped notes will be heard if the intonation is accurate. It is beneficial to practice these double-stops with and without vibrato.

When you play a fifth the bass tone will sound an octave lower than the lower note of the fifth. If you play a fourth you hear the bass tone two octaves lower than the upper note of the fourth.

The player should become accustomed to testing these intervals by listening to the resultant bass tones when double-stops are played.

Q. Exactly how should we teach a student to develop accurate intonation in double-stops?

A. If a student plays a double-stop and one of the notes is out of tune, ask the student:
1. if that double-stop is in tune;
2. if it is not in tune, which note is out of tune, and;
3. if it is too high or too low.

If you play a double-stop out of tune, and correct it and go ahead, very little value is gained. You cannot correct the intonation of a double-stop and then go ahead. You must play it correctly a few times. You should memorize exactly what adjustment you made to play it in tune. When you play that note or double-stop again, the subconscious mind frequently comes to your rescue and helps you make the proper adjustment. Memory plays an important part in the development of good intonation.

If you constantly accept notes that are slightly out of tune, you may become too tolerant of faulty intonation.

The Art and Science of Playing Double Stops

Q. How soon should students play on two strings simultaneously?

A. Actually, in the first few lessons the students should memorize the sensation of playing on a level where two strings can be sounded at the same time.

Q. When we start double stops that early, are students more likely to play on two strings when they mean to play on only one string?

A. In my opinion, the reverse is true. When they memorize the sensation of the level between two strings, they are more likely to be successful in avoiding sounding two strings when they want to play on a single string. Double stops can actually be started on open strings in the first few weeks of study.

Q. Is that helpful in learning to tune the violin later on?

A. Yes. Early in their training they memorize the sound of the perfect fifth.

Q. Do you suggest that students in their early training play double stops also with the fingers?

A. Yes, I do. This skill should be developed by rote. As soon as the pupils learn to keep the first finger on a string, and play the next lower open string, they are then memorizing the sensation of playing double stops. The second, third, and fourth fingers can also be played in the same way. Here is an example:

Do this on all strings.

Q. How soon should we teach the pupil to cover two strings with the same finger?

A. Well toward the end of the first year. It could be taken up as a special rote game where we say to the pupil, "Place the first finger on the D string in the first position, and the first finger on the A string. Now, try to play them both at the same time. Can you keep the finger down on both strings?"

It may be helpful to place the first finger between the strings. You may have to flatten the first finger just a bit.

But one thing is clear: It is of extreme importance that pupils learn to play this perfect fifth. It makes it possible to develop velocity and to go from one string to another smoothly with greater accuracy.

Q. In general, what are the problems in learning how to play double stops?

A. The first problem is to shape the hand in such a way that each note will be clearly articulated; the second is to find the correct bow level; the third is to avoid applying too much additional bow weight in order to sound both strings. It is the bow arm level that is to be adjusted.

You must encourage pupils to test notes with the open strings as soon as possible.

Since the lower note is a thicker string, there may be some advantage if the bow leans slightly more toward the lower string.

Q. What exercises have you to develop double-stop skills in the first position?

A. Here is a set of 25 small etudes in the first position. They are to be practiced softly and slowly. The two strings must be sounded simultaneously throughout. The pupils must listen carefully and try to decide if each double stop is in tune. If they are not sure, adjust the fingers until they are certain that they are in tune. They must be very patient.

After they are able to play the first five lines, the teacher may add a new one and remove one.

Learn to play these double stops without adding additional bow pressure.
(1) Practice softly and slowly. (2) The two strings must be heard throughout. Aim for smooth, even tones. (3) Master each line before proceeding to the next.

52

Q. What comments can you make about playing thirds in the first position?

A. Here we meet with an interesting problem. Both fingers have to be placed on the strings at the same time. One finger may be a bit more sluggish than the other and will have to be hurried a bit.

Q. Suppose a pupil cannot place the fourth finger easily?

A. A suggestion that will be helpful is to slightly bend the left wrist inward toward the neck of the violin. I say this because some pupils, as they play the D and the F in the following example, have a tendency to allow the wrist to move outward, making it more difficult.

Q. What are some of the difficulties in playing fourths?

A. Here we have a similar problem. In the following example one finger has to go from one string to another, while the other finger is merely dropped on the string. The finger that moves from one string to another must be kept as close as possible to the string so that both notes will sound simultaneously.

Q. What are the problems in playing perfect fifths?

A. Perfect fifths present another problem. The width of the fingers and the way one places the fingers on the string are to be taken into consideration. Some players find it easier to think of just placing the finger between the strings. Some of the time, however, a slight adjustment of the finger placement and the left elbow is required. (I am assuming that the strings are not false.)

Q. How can one tell if the string is false?

A. The first test is whether you can play perfect fifths with only a slight adjustment of the fingers or elbow or both. When I say adjustment of the elbow, I mean moving it a bit more to the left or to the right. The following is a good test for the lower strings, but not for the E string: Pluck the string firmly and note the way it vibrates. If it vibrates as one whole unit from the nut to the bridge, the chances are that it is not false. If one part of the string vibrates and another little section of it vibrates separately, it is a good indication that the string is false.

Q. Do you have any suggestions about the performance of sixths?

A. The only thing I can say about sixths is that you must be careful to make sure that both notes sound simultaneously when going from one sixth to another. There is a tendency for one note to sound first. You must determine which finger is late and move that finger faster. It means that there are two different speeds in finger action. Bearing this in mind will be helpful.

Q. Why are octaves so difficult to play in tune?

A. I don't think they are more difficult than any other form of double stop, but when an octave is out of tune it is more discernible to the listener. The important thing here is to concentrate on the first finger. As a result of our training there is a relationship between the first finger and the fourth finger, which forms a frame for the left hand. When the first finger is in tune, the fourth finger is more likely to be in tune.

Octaves are absolutely essential in the building of a sound left-hand technic. It is very obvious on the violin and viola that the octave represents an interval of a perfect fourth except that the fourth finger is on the next string. Every string player knows that each higher position requires the gradual lessening of the distances between the first and fourth fingers. It is this requirement that poses a definite problem in accuracy in intonation.

If the octave is in tune, the other fingers will more likely fall into place. As soon as the player learns to adjust the first and fourth fingers automatically to the narrowing of the intervals, ascending, and the widening of them while descending, accuracy of pitch is practically assured in all positions.

Very frequently, when playing octaves, one is apt to over-estimate the distance of a half-step shift.

Q. How soon should we start the study of tenths?

A. As soon as the pupil can play octaves reasonably well. Here the important thing to concentrate on is the first finger. A new dimension is added when we realize that frequently the first finger will ascend a full step while the fourth finger will ascend only a half-step, and vice versa. The pupil must bear this in mind at all times.

Q. Suppose a student finds it difficult to stretch a tenth?

A. Then the student must practice an exercise which will be conducive to widening the web between the first and the fourth fingers. I will suggest the following exercise. Encourage your students to create additional exercises based on the following example:

When you play tenths, it is easier to reach back with the first finger than to extend the fourth finger.

The weight of the hand must be set in favor of the fourth finger. I would suggest that the practicing of octaves and tenths be limited to ten minute intervals, followed by working on something completely different. You may then go back to tenths two or three times a day.

Octaves can be slightly harmful if a nerve at the tip of the first finger becomes sensitive.

There is a tonal problem in playing tenths. Since there is a big difference in pitch between the lower and the upper notes, the lane that the bow will travel in has to be adjusted so that you get the best quality of tone when they are played as a double stop.

When you play the upper note alone, draw the bow closer to the bridge, but when you play a tenth, a very slight compromise must be made to accomodate the lower note.

Q. What comments would you make on the practicing of fingered octaves?

A. First, I would like to say that fingered octaves are extremely important. Octave passages that move with some degree of velocity are more frequently played as fingered octaves rather than with the first and fourth fingers. When playing fingered octaves the player must memorize the sensation of reaching back slightly with the first finger and second finger. When this is done the tip of the second finger should always face the bridge.

I find that many students are likely to play the second finger a bit too high and the third finger a bit too low. It is the second finger that should be tested as frequently as possible with open strings.

Q. What general suggestions have you to offer regarding the practicing of double stops of any interval?

A. First, test as many notes as possible. Next, try to memorize the distance between the fingers. For example, there is a tendency for pupils , when they play major thirds, to make the fourth finger a bit too high in the third position.

For example:

A very good way to practice a passage in all forms of double stops is to use both fingers for the double stops but to sound only the lower notes with the bow. Do this a few times, then repeat the same double stops, using both fingers, but sounding only the upper notes. You then practice the passage sounding both notes.

Bear in mind that memory plays an important part in the development of good intonation, particularly in double stops. You might say to the student, "When you play a double stop out of tune, make the proper adjustments until you are sure it is in tune. Which finger did you have to raise? Which finger did you have to lower? You must memorize whatever adjustments you had to make."

When you play it correctly a few times, you are more likely to play it in tune the next day than if you had just corrected it and had gone ahead. You must memorize what you did to correct that double stop. If corrections are made in this way, your subconscious memory will aid in your performance.

Q. Have you any suggestions to develop good intonation while shifting?

A. When you shift from one double stop to another, it will be helpful to concentrate on one finger during the shift, and that should be the easiest finger for the ear to judge in terms of intonation.

In the following example it might be the first finger:

Q. In the following example, which finger should I concentrate on?

A. Here you should concentrate on the second finger, C$^\#$, because it is the finger that is not changed. In other words, you should concentrate on the unchanged finger.

Q. In this next example, would you also concentrate on the second finger?

A. Yes, but for another reason. It is the finger nearest to the new finger, and that is the finger you should concentrate on . Here, it is the second finger which should direct the shift.

Q. How about the quality of sound in double stopping?

A. To develop a beautiful quality of sound in double stopping, you must adjust the level of the right arm in order to sound both strings simultaneously and to avoid forcing the tone. Bear in mind also, that the lower string is thicker and that the bow should be inclined more toward the lower string.

All double stops should be practiced at different dynamic levels. You must play in the proper lane on the string, carefully considering the speed and pressure as you draw the bow.

Q. When shifting with double stops do we apply the same rules as we do for single stops?

A. Yes. To a great extent the rules are the same.

Ex. No. 1

In Exercise No. 1, you shift from the first position to the third position with the same fingers. The problem here is simple and limited to intonation and to the ease with which the shift is made. A slight additional head or jaw pressure is applied to the violin or viola during the shift so that the left hand can move up and down freelv.

Ex. No. 2

In Exercise No. 2, you shift to different fingers from the first to the third position. However, since the notes are in a slur, you will shift with the two fingers that are on the strings. That is, you shift (ascend) with the first and third fingers. When you arrive in the third position, the second and fourth fingers are dropped on to the strings. If it is an espressive shift, you will want to vibrate as soon as you arrive at the new double stop. In that case you will lift the lower fingers as soon as you strike the upper notes. You always descend with the fingers that are already on the strings.

Q. How do you shift to another double stop when they are in separate bows?

A. When they are in separate bows, the rule is that you shift with the fingers that you are going to.

In this example you shift with the second and fourth fingers. I will repeat that when you descend, you always shift with the fingers that are already on the strings.

Q. What is the rule when you shift (ascend) in a scale line from two higher fingers to two lower fingers, in this example from a 2 and 4 to 1 and 3?

A. The general rule is that you ascend with the fingers that you are going to, whether they are in a slur or in separate bows.

In the example above you shift to the third position with the first and third fingers. However, when you shift slowly for expressive purposes, it is possible for the second and fourth fingers to start the shift and an instant later the first and third fingers will displace the second and fourth fingers.

On the way down, or in the descending shifts, you always shift with the fingers that are already on the strings.

Q. How about crossing strings in the same position when you play double stops?

A. When you cross strings in double stops, it is advisable to think about choosing the finger that you will use as a pivot so that you can acquire a smooth connection. The pivoting finger is sounded alone for an instant, but it is so short that the ear is unaware that only one note is sounded. To the listener it sounds as though the two notes have been sounded simultaneously.

The following example shows the way to use one note as a pivot in the same position:

In this exercise the note C is the pivot note.

Q. How about shifting and crossing strings at the same time when you play double stops?

A. Always find the most convenient note which will be used as the pivot. It will be helpful for a smooth transition from one double stop to another.

In the following example, the pivotal note is E.

Q. What are some of the principles involved in playing three or four voice chords?

A. In Exercise No. 3, you have three- and four-voice chords as they are written and, then as they are played, when the dynamic marks are either piano, mezzo piano, or mezzo forte.

The length of the lower grace notes is dependent on the effect you wish to get. The important thing to remember is that to get good tone quality you must change lanes.

When you break the chord, the two lower notes are played near the fingerboard. It might be in the first or second lanes. However, when you sustain the two upper notes, the bow must travel in a higher lane, closer to the bridge.

Through experimentation you can find exactly the right lane to get the best tone quality, depending on how loudly or softly you play.

Q. How do you play four-voice chords in forte or fortissimo?

A. When you play chords in forte or fortissimo, you must strike the three lower notes simultaneously.

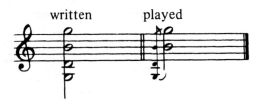

The quality of the chords depends on how straight the bow is drawn and how quickly you find the right lane for the two upper notes that are sustained.

In general, chords may be practiced in triplets as in Exercise No. 4.

Ex. No. 4

Q. What suggestions can you offer when we play a series of chords?

A. This involves sensations that are mental and physical. You must be psychologically prepared to quickly direct the fingers to the next chord by thinking ahead. Some chords may be more easily played by bending the left wrist slghtly inward toward the neck of the instrument. It is a matter of mental and physical preparedness.

Q. How do you play three-voice chords simultaneously?

A. Set the bow firmly into the middle string of the chord about an inch from the frog as you would play a martelé note. Draw the bow quickly and release this pressure at the same time, using about five inches of bow. Lift the bow, and in a quick circular motion draw the bow back to the frog and play the next chord.

Some General Principles of Fingerings

Q. What are some of the guidelines in the choice of fingering?

A. Passages are fingered in accordance with three musical components:

    1. rhythm

    2. phrase

    3. dynamics

From the musical standpoint fingering is very creative. You must consider the emotional message of the composer, the style of the interpretation, and the period in which the music is written.

Fingering is not only creative, but very individual. A personal choice of fingering is sometimes based more on the comfort of the player than on any rationale. You must consider a person's technical equipment, size and flexibility of the hand.

Q. How would fingerings be affected by rhythm?

A. Take rhythmic groups such as triplets or four sixteenth notes. Your object should be to try to play them on the same string, if possible.

A group such as an eighth and two sixteenth notes might be better played on the same string rather than changing strings on the sixteenths. A general rule is to play many phrases or parts of phrases on the same string in order to maintain the same tone color. This will also apply to the last few notes of many phrases.

Q. Would extensions be helpful in maintaining the same tone color or remaining on the same string?

A. Yes. When it is a moving passage and not played too loudly, extensions are very helpful.

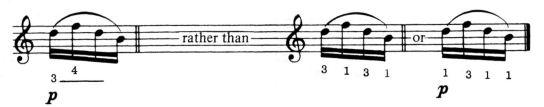

An interesting type of fingering is where you go to another position without shifting. You stretch into it, and once you have played the note, the hand follows.

stretch   hand follows

Q. What fingerings should be used for augmented seconds?

A. When playing augmented seconds you have two choices:

    1. using adjacent fingers;

    2. skipping a finger.

The advantage in skipping a finger is that the frame of the hand remains the same. That is to be carefully considered, especially in rapid passages where you can get more velocity and greater accuracy of intonation.

preferred

Q. May I have an example of how the dynamic mark will affect the fingering?

A. If you are playing fortissimo, it might be preferable to play phrases or parts of phrases on the E string for greater brilliance rather than shifting up on the A string.

Q. In the rather early stages of string playing what general suggestions can you offer as to when to shift?

A. Many times it is best to shift on half-steps. I would suggest that you shift on a strong beat so that there is a rhythmic impulse that is supplied by the shift itself. Plan shifts so as to avoid accents which are not desirable. Shifts that occur on a change of bow stroke are always acceptable. The most important guideline, however, is the musical content of the work.

Here are two examples of when you should use either the fourth finger or the open string.

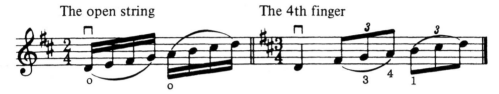

In rapid scale passages the open strings are often preferable because they provide greater clarity; you will then disregard the rhythmic grouping.

Q. Will the vibrato affect the choice of fingering?

A. By all means. Many players will produce a better quality of sound when they vibrate on a particular finger. With many it is the second or third finger.

Q. Is it advisable to use the third finger instead of the fourth finger in singing passages where the notes are held for a length of time?

A. I would think that in long, prominent notes the third finger might produce a better sound, however, I hesitate to make this a general rule. Each instance should be decided on an individual basis. Many performers feel they can vibrate more freely with the third finger.

If a fourth finger has been well trained in the early stages, and if it is reasonably strong, it can supply all the finger pressure required on the string to clearly articulate the note. We sometimes sacrifice the efficiency of the fourth finger by not using it enough.

A well-balanced hand is one with a strong fourth finger. We weaken it by constantly using the other fingers in its place. When the tempo permits, I like the idea of changing fingers on some repeated notes.

Vibrato

Q. How would you define the ideal vibrato?

A. The ideal vibrato is a combination of the finger, hand, and arm. The flexibility of the first joint (nearest the fingertip) is essential for the development of a good vibrato. An advanced player takes into account the speed and intensity of each.

Q. When is the best time to start teaching the vibrato?

A. The general rule is that when the left hand of the pupil is reasonably well-set, the vibrato may be started.

On the other hand, there is the psychological factor. Some pupils want to start earlier. In that case you can give them a set of preparatory exercises. I would say that after they have had the third position for a few weeks, the vibrato may be started.

I prefer, however, to wait until they have also done some shifting studies between the first and third positions. Occasionally pupils may start the vibrato in the first position if they are very impatient.

Q. What exercises would you give the pupil before starting with the actual vibrato?

A. The exercises are mechanical. They are in the form of calisthenics, and are performed without the instrument.

Hold your left arm in playing position (without the instrument) with the hand as high as the shoulder and the arm as relaxed as possible.

Shake the left hand energetically a number of times in varous directions, in circles, clock-wise and counter clock-wise, moving the hand back and forth in a regular rhythm. Now snap the wrist as if shaking water off the fingers.

Q. When you move the hand back and forth from the wrist joint, do you move it as far as you can?

A. Yes, I would exaggerate that motion just to gain flexibility.

Q. How long should the student do these preparatory exercises before starting the actual vibrato on the violin itself?

A. I would say a few weeks, because these exercises also involve rhythmic control. Whatever motion there is in the forearm will only be sympathetic. We want to concentrate on the hand in the wrist joint and on the muscles actively involved. The player's attention must not wander. Many artists do these exercises regularly.

Q. What different types of vibrato are there?

A. The hand vibrato, the arm vibrato, and the finger vibrato.

With the hand vibrato there is a sympathetic motion of the forearm. With the arm vibrato there is a sympathetic motion of the upper arm. With the finger vibrato there is sympathetic motion of the hand.

Q. Which one would you teach first?

A. Here we have different opinions. I prefer to start with the hand vibrato. It is easier and has a way of insuring a correct function of the left hand.

Teachers who have fine arm vibratos are very likely to be more successful in first teaching the arm vibrato.

The next step is to discipline the shaking of the left hand in the following manner: shake the wrist slowly and evenly in eighth notes; start from a position where the hand and arm form a straight line; imagine that you have placed the second finger on the D or A strings, playing F$^\#$ or C$^\#$.

From this position roll the hand from the wrist joint backward toward the scroll. Pupils who can do this for a length of time in even eighth notes will be well on the road to developing a well-disciplined left hand. A week or two later this exercise may be done in triplets, in dotted eighths and sixteenths, and then in sixteenths and dotted eighths. If pupils can do these exercises in even sixteenths without any wavering of the rhythm, they may then be started on the violin itself.

Q. What about the flexibility of the finger joints of the left hand?

A. That is very important. Hold the arm up as in the previous exercise. The tip of the first finger is placed on the inner edge of the thumb. Bend the first joint of the first finger inward and outward in a quick snap. Do this with each finger for a number of weeks even after the vibrato has been started on the instrument.

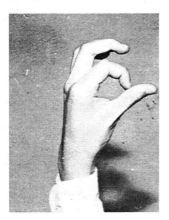 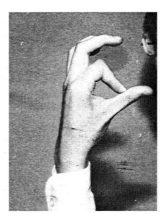

Q. How do we start learning the vibrato on the instrument?

A. Play the note A in the third position, second finger on the D string. The lower part of the palm of the hand must touch the body of the violin. I like to have the hand more to the right of the neck, as though playing in the fourth position. (For private pupils there is some advantage in starting the vibrato in the fourth position.)

We must make sure that the left thumb is opposite the first finger or slightly behind it. However, many students are successful with the thumb placed between the first and second fingers.

Q. What part of the thumb should contact the neck?

A. For many pupils it is best for the thumb to contact the neck midway between the first joint and the tip of the thumb. I must emphasize, however, that the placement of the thumb is a variable.

Do not permit the thumb to hook around the side of the neck. I personally prefer the tip of the thumb to point slightly toward the scroll.

Q. What about the base knuckle of the first finger?

A. The base knuckle should leave the neck. The side of the knuckle of the first finger must not touch the neck during these oscillation exercises.

Q. Why would you start with the second finger?

A. We start with the second finger because it is easier to keep the base knuckle of the first finger from touching the neck. The finger must be placed in an upright position.

Q. Just how would you tell the student to proceed?

A. I would say, " Roll the finger tip from this upright position to slightly backward in an elongated position slightly below the pitch of the note. Do this in even eighth notes. These exercises should be done first without the bow and then with the bow. Draw the bow for four slow beats. The note itself and the lowering of the note constitute a beat. The rolling (back away from body) can be exaggerated so that the finger flattens out, and it can be done in a vigorous manner from the start. But do not allow the knuckle to collapse.

During this rolling motion of the finger tip the finger actually remains in the same spot. The heel of the hand must continue to lightly touch the rib of the instrument. Think of a rocking chair that rocks back and forth on the same spot. As soon as you are able to do this in even eighth notes, repeat the same exercise, oscillating in a gentle manner from the primary note to a bit below."

During this first exercise you must be aware of the following:

1. that this oscillation or rolling motion must be done quite parallel to the string. Actually, it is not exactly in the direction of the string. It is really a slightly oblique motion, but you must feel the sensation of doing it in the direction of the string. You are not to allow the string to be pulled to either side;
2. that the knuckle must not collapse;
3. that the left thumb, entire hand and arm should be more relaxed than usual. This relaxation should actually come from the shoulder joint;
4. that you are to avoid applying too much finger pressure on the string — only enough to clearly articulate the sound;
5. that the side of the first finger is not permitted to touch the neck during the oscillation;
6. that the third and fourth fingers do not fall into the palm of the hand or under the fingerboard.

Start with eighth notes, four beats to a bow, then six, then eight beats.

You must avoid a natural tendency for the tip of the bow to slide toward the fingerboard during this exercise.

Q. How soon should the same exercises be done with the third finger?

A. This may vary with each student. It might be after a week or two.

Q. What happens to the second finger when the third finger is started?

A. The second finger must leave the string. Do not allow two fingers to remain on the string for these exercises. The fourth and the first fingers will follow.

Q. Why do you leave the first finger till last?

A. When you do these exercises with the first finger, there is a tendency to allow the side of the first finger to touch the neck. This must be avoided. You must make sure that the hand is a little more to the right of the neck to permit greater freedom to oscillate. Your motto should be "Left Wrist to the Right of the Neck."

Q. When vibrating with the fourth finger, what shape should the first finger assume?

A. The first finger may be slightly curved with the tip pointing upwards or a bit toward the scroll. It must be quite relaxed. However, the tip of the third finger will be close and slightly pointed to the fourth finger.

Q. What tempo should be used for these exercises?

A. Circa ♩ = M.M. 66

Q. After each finger has completed these exercises, what is the next step?

A. You then increase the speed of the oscillation by playing sixteenth notes, four beats to a bow, and by lessening the width of the oscillation. You now have the additional challenge of moving the bow much slower.

Q. When one is able to discipline the movement of the hand in an even manner without any fluctuation of the rhythm, what would the next step be?

A. Various combinations of rhythms should be introduced. The following examples will serve as a guide.

The arrows (↓) indicate a slight lowering of the pitch.

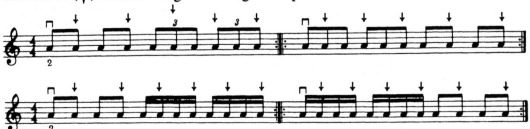

More combinations may be added.

Q. At this point, would it be possible to apply the vibrato to a simple piece?

A. Yes, by all means. Write out a sixteen-bar melody in the third position using whole notes and some quarter notes. If possible, improvise a piano accompaniment or a second violin part to be used at lessons. They could be recorded on a cassette for home use, in the classroom, or in the studio. At this stage it is best for the pupil not to vibrate on the quarter notes.

Q. Should the heel of the hand still be in contact with the rib of the instrument?

A. Yes. Now ask the pupils to play sixteenth notes, drawing each bow for eight beats.

Q. Suppose the pupils have difficulty playing eight beats in one bow?

A. Try the psychological gesture of asking them to count eight beats in a half bow. Pupils must learn to move the bow slowly. They also have a tendency to move the bow too quickly at the beginning of each bow stroke.

Many students tend to hold their breath during this exercise. They should all learn to take a slight breath at the beginning of each bow stroke.

Q. What do we do when the pupils allow the tip of the bow to slide toward the fingerboard?

A. As they approach the tip, there must be a feeling of the bow being drawn away from the body, and on the up-bow of being drawn closer to the body.

The pupils must realize that while playing in the upper half of the bow, the right elbow moves slightly forward.

Q. What other materials or pieces do you use for the vibrato study?

A. All etudes and pieces in the third position should incorporate the vibrato on the long notes.

$$(o - d. - d)$$

We try to gradually increase the speed of the oscillation until it is a normal vibrato. However, it is advisable for the student to have a vibrato on the slow side for a length of time, rather than on the fast side.

Q. When do we start the vibrato in the first position?

A. Before we do that, ask the student to play the same pieces in the third position, but keeping the heel of the hand about a half inch away from the rib of the violin. If they can do that and still vibrate in the same manner without the use of the upper arm, it will not be difficult to transfer the vibrato to the first position.

Q. If the students cannot vibrate easily with the heel of the hand away from the rib of the violin, do we still start the vibrato in the first position?

A. Yes, but we go through the same rhythmic procedure in the first position that we did in the third position. However, in the first position there are only two points of contact: the tip of the finger and the left thumb. Make sure that the base knuckle of the first finger does not touch the neck. The expression I like to use is "Make sure the left hand is always to the right of the neck." The tip of the vibrating finger should face the left side of the player's face.

Q. In what position do you start the arm vibrato?

A. In the first position so that the heel of hand does not touch the instrument.

Q. When you use the arm vibrato, do you still vibrate only below the note?

A. Yes, only below the note, but this does not necessarily apply to the cello or the bass.

Q. Is there a difference between the violin-viola vibrato and the cello-bass vibrato?

A. The procedure on the violin and viola should be the same, but the intense rapid vibrato should never to used on the viola. It should be wider and perhaps a bit slower.

For the cello and bass the impulse should come from the elbow joint. It is actually a well coordinated movement of the forearm and fingers. There will be some sympathetic movement of the upper arm.

Q. Suppose a pupil comes to you who already has an arm vibrato and no hand or wrist vibrato? What do you suggest to the pupil?

A. I would certainly allow the arm vibrato to be used. That should be the one used most of the time if it produces a beautiful sound. I would then attempt to develop a hand vibrato to go along with it.

Q. How do you develop a finger vibrato?

A. We now concentrate mostly on the oscillation of the finger itself. There is a slight sympathetic motion of the hand. It is used mostly when you are playing morendo or diminuendo during a ritard. It is also used when vibrating in eighth-note passages. When the notes are too fast to vibrate on each, you use a slight finger vibrato. It is also used to highlight certain eighth notes.

Q. How would you teach the finger vibrato?

A. I don't believe it requires any specific teaching. Just concentrate on the finger oscillation.

With the finger vibrato, a little more flesh of the tip of the finger is applied to the string. When there is a series of eighth notes you vibrate on every note or on every second, third, or fourth note, depending on the rhythm or the tempo. This gives the effect of a continuous vibrato.

Q. Is there a general rule as to when the various types of vibrato are used?

A. Yes. There are different types of vibrato with different speeds to express various moods. The vibrato must fit the mood of each musical phrase.

In catilena passages you might use the hand vibrato. When the music becomes more intense you gradually apply the arm vibrato. The arm vibrato may be used on three- or four-voice chords or on single notes that are very intense.

Q. When do you use no vibrato at all?

A. There are certain passages of great tranquility in slow movements where you want a different type of sound. Tones without any vibrato may be referred to as "white tones." The vibrato is gradually introduced as the passage becomes louder and more intense or dramatic.

An example of starting without vibrato may be found in the following: Play the first three eighth notes broadly without vibrato. The next note, E, could start pianissimo on a white tone and the vibrato gradually introduced as a crescendo is made on that note.

Handel, *Sonata in D*

Q. What do we do when a student has a vibrato that is too slow?

A. The vibrato may also be sped up by vibrating on whole bow quarter notes using the martelé stroke. The object is to encourage the hand to get as many oscillations as possible within the length of that quarter note. It is a good way to speed up the vibrato. Another goal of this exercise is to lessen the width of the oscillations and to relax the entire arm. Lightening the finger pressure on the string will frequently be very helpful. Vibrating as quickly as possible in short spurts such as fast eighth notes with a long pause, after each note, may be very helpful.

When the vibrato is too wide, the chances are that the student is oscillating above the note as well as below. The sensation to memorize is that the primary note itself can be likened to a fence or a wall, and the player cannot go beyond it when vibrating.

I want to stress that in the vibrato the first joint must be very flexible.

Sometimes the vibrato can become contagious. Ask a pupil who has a very slow vibrato to play with one who has a fast vibrato. You might be surprised at the results.

Q. What can be done for a student who has a vibrato that is too rapid?

A. This is sometimes called a "nervous vibrato." To avoid this, the student should practice daily the slow rhythms that were suggested for starting the vibrato, while allowing the scroll of the violin to lightly touch the wall.

Try widening the amplitude of the oscillation as well as permitting the left thumb to leave the neck for practice purposes.

Q. What suggestions have you when vibrating in the high positions?

A. Above the sixth position the amplitude of the vibrato should be narrowed because of the gradual lessening of the distance between pitches. In the very high positions, such as the tenth position, it may be helpful to avoid vibrating on the finger that is on the string and to vibrate on the fingers that are over the string.

It may become a bit easier if you move the instrument a bit to the left in the very high positions.

Q. Why do some string players find it difficult to sustain the vibrato when going from one note to another?

A. For many players the "vibrato sostenuto" is a skill that will require some practice. In the following example play the first note, G, with a vibrato that is quite relaxed. Count slowly. On the third beat place the third finger on F# while you continue to play and vibrate on the note, G.

In the next measure gently remove the note G so that the vibrato will blend in the note, F#. Do the same with the third and second fingers, and the same with the second and first fingers. With this exercise it will be easier to memorize the sensation of blending the vibrato from one note to another.

This is what I call the "finger legato." That means transferring the vibrato motion from one finger to another without interruption. The vibrato is so important to the technique of the left hand that I might call it an essential part of a good left-hand technique. It is important that the whole hand and arm be posed on the vibrating finger. That means that the arm and hand are balanced on that finger. The matter of connecting two or more notes without any interruption of the vibrato can be accomplished only by transferring the balance of the hand from one finger to another.

Q. How would you introduce the vibrato in double stops?

A. I would start by playing slow double stops scales in thirds, sixths, octaves, fingered octaves, and tenths.

Try to vibrate freely by relaxing the arm and hand. The elementary double-stop studies on pages 51 and 52 will provide good material for the vibrato.

Q. What sensation should the player feel when vibrating on double stops?

A. When playing double stops it is actually wrong to have the feeling of the hand being balanced equally on the two fingers.

Q. How would you describe the correct feeling?

A. The correct feeling is that the hand should be balanced on only one finger when playing double stops.

Q. Which finger should that be?

A. The balance of the left hand should always be on the higher finger, never the lower finger. The higher finger does not necessarily mean the higher note.

There are fine players who vibrate well on single notes. However, the moment they play thirds with the second and fourth fingers, tenths or fingered octaves, that freedom seems to disappear. The vibrato is affected, and they seem to have that "locked in" feeling.

Q. Can you give us an example?

A. Let's take an easy double stop in the first position (a major third, with the first finger on the D string, note E, and the third finger on the G string, note C). The correct feeling should be that the player is vibrating with the balance of the hand on the third finger. The first finger should vibrate sympathetically with the third finger. The balance of the hand is on the higher finger, which, in this case, is the lower note.

Q. Can you give another example of how that would work out?

A. Let's try an experiment. Play the note E on the D string with the first finger, and vibrate on it. While you are vibrating on that note and without stopping, add the C on the G string with the third finger. Try holding these two notes until you study the sensation in your hand. What does it feel like?

Now do just the opposite. Vibrate on the G string with the third finger, note C. Then add E, first finger on the D string, which means that the balance of the hand remains on the third finger. Study this new feeling while playing both notes.

If you do this correctly, you will discover that in the second instance, when you added the first finger you have the feeling that the hand is much freer and the tone is richer.

This should prove to you that the weight or balance of the hand should be on the higher finger, even though it may be the lower note.

Q. Are there any double stops that may be played with arm vibrato?

A. Yes. The three-voice chords, for example, where the notes are very short or intense, such as in a chord played with the martelé stroke.

Q. I find it much easier to vibrate with my second and third fingers. How can I improve the ease and quality of my first and fourth finger vibrato?

A. You must make a study of each finger and try to determine just what you must do to beautify the vibrato on the first and fourth fingers. Vibrate with the finger that produces the best sound. For example, the second finger in the third position on the D string, note A.

Vibrate for a number of bows, holding each stroke for eight beats. Play the same note with the third finger (second position). With many players both notes will be equally beautiful as far as the vibrato is concerned.

Now play the same note with the first finger in the fourth position. Experiment with the first finger vibrato so that, in time, it will match and be as beautiful as the second and third finger vibrato.

You might find that a little less finger pressure on the string will help. You might also try changing the angle of the finger on the string.

Play the same note with the fourth finger in the first position. The object is to match the vibrato with the first and fourth fingers with the vibrato of the second and third fingers.

Q. Can you recommend a specific number of oscillations per note to develop a beautiful vibrato?

A. To develop a rich, warm vibrato consider adopting the following procedure:

1. practice any scale, holding each note for five seconds, then four seconds, then three seconds, then two, and then one second;
2. vibrate by oscillating five times to the five second note; then five times to the four second note; then five times to the three second note; then five times to the two second note; then five times to the one second note.

Eventually oscillate approximately five times to each note that is one second in duration. That may well be considered a good speed for a fine vibrato.

Developing a Fine Bow Arm
The Basic Skills

Q. What is the main challenge in the development of a good bow arm?

A. Avoiding bad habits.

Q. Have you any suggestions to avoid the development of bad habits?

A. We really cannot avoid them unless every practice period is carefully supervised. In a general way we should, in our teaching, try to have the pupil memorize the correct sensations for developing the various skills and avoiding the main faults.

Q. What are the main faults?

A. They are:
1. the lack of ability to draw a straight bow;
2. failure to memorize the sensation of freedom of movement from the frog to the middle of the bow — the arm should move freely and lightly in the shoulder joint, as though the entire arm is airborne;
3. the failure of the little finger to regulate the amount of bow weight required as the frog is approached (the little finger is a key factor in withholding some of the bow weight, applying only as much as needed);
4. failure to open and close the lower arm in the elbow joint when playing from two to three inches below the middle to the very tip; the sensation to memorize is that the elbow joint is like a well oiled hinge;
5. failure to move the elbow slightly forward as the tip of the bow is approached — when playing at the tip the frog should be a bit farther away from the player's body — the little finger should be placed on the inside of the stick, more toward the palm rather than on the very top of the bow;
6. failure to apply more hair on the string as the bow approaches the tip;
7. failure to transmit additional weight through the first finger to the stick when playing above the middle of the bow;
8. failure to memorize the relationship between the weight and the speed of the bow;
9. failure to establish the best point of contact on the string, i.e. the best lane in which to draw the bow;
10. a tendency to allow the bow arm to become tense and to raise the shoulder in the joint as the bow reaches the frog

Q. What do you consider to be a good how hold?

A. When playing at the frog the thumb is flexible and bent outward. The little finger is placed on the stick in a curved shape. For practical reasons it might be advisable for the tip of the little finger to contact the stick a bit closer to the palm of the hand, rather than on the very top of the stick. However, there are many fine performers who perfer to place the tip of the little finger on the very top of the bow.

Q. How are the other fingers to be placed?

A. The third finger should be placed toward the pearl on the frog. If the fingers are long, it might even cover the pearl. The second finger should be wrapped around the bow in such a way that the tip of the thumb might point approximately toward the first crease of the middle (second) finger. I am referring now to the crease nearest the tip of the middle finger.

The first finger should contact the stick in what I call "the neutral position" which is midway between the first joint and the middle joint.

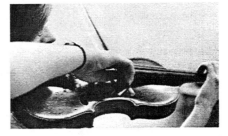

Photo No. 18A   **Photo No. 18B**

Q. Is this neutral position to be constant?

A. No. It is variable. Actually, the distance between the first joint and the middle joint might be considered an area where we can go from one joint to another. It might be considered a sliding area.

Q. In what way is it variable?

A. Consider these guidelines. For long, drawn out bows in fortissimo, the finger might contact the stick more toward the first joint. For the springing strokes, such as the various forms of the spiccato and the sautillé, it might be best for the first finger to contact the stick between the two joints.

For the martelé strokes and the solid detaché, contacting the stick at the middle joint might produce better results. That is why it is a variable. This does not, however, apply to all players. It is certainly beneficial to constantly experiment with the different contacts.

Q. How should the thumb be placed?

A. The right side of the tip of the thumb should contact the edge of the frog so that part of the thumb is in contact with the frog and part of the thumb is in contact with the stick itself. This is also variable, depending on the size of the hand. Some players take the liberty of placing the thumb on the stick about ⅛ or ¼ inch from the frog.

I would like to make one more comment about a good bow hold. We might describe the hold as being involved with two contact points and a sliding area where weight is applied. One contact point is the tip of the little finger. The other is the tip of the thumb on the stick. The sliding area is between the first and second knuckles of the first finger.

Q. How do you teach memorizing the sensation of a good bow hold?

A. In the following manner:

1. hold the right hand up and spread the fingers apart as wide as possible, Photo 19;

2. curve the fingers — this immediately relaxes the right hand, Photo 20;

3. place the tip of the thumb in the first crease of the middle (second) finger, Photo 21;

4. turn the lower right arm inward in a rotary motion from the elbow joint, Photo 22;

5. take a dowel about 11 inches long (a chop stick or pencil) — hold the dowel in the left hand, with the point of the dowel facing the ceiling, Photo 22;

Photo No. 19   **Photo No. 20**

Photo No. 21   **Photo No. 22**

6. in this position place the right hand so that it touches the side of the dowel — the tip of the thumb is to remain in the first crease of the middle finger, Photo 23;

7. With the hand touching the side of the dowel, move it up and down a number of times from the wrist joint in slow motion — the right elbow must remain quiet during this process, Photo 24;

Photo No. 23   **Photo No. 24**

8. now hold the dowel horizontally so that the tip faces to the left; the feeling is that it is still an up and down motion.

Q. How can the pupil memorize the sensation of drawing a straight bow above the middle?

A. By learning to open and close the right elbow joint. The elbow must stay in line with the right side of the player's body. With the dowel pressing lightly into the elbow joint, open and close the elbow without moving the upper arm. Photo 25.

Q. How do you teach the proper method of holding of the bow?

A. By using the following nine steps, which can be found in the *Applebaum String Method* or in *The Young String Student*:

Photo No. 25

1. hold the bow at the frog on the screw with your left hand, the hair facing you, and the tip of the bow pointing toward the ceiling, Photo 26;

2. wiggle the right thumb vigorously;

3. bend the right thumb and place the right side of the tip of the thumb on the corner of the frog on the underside of the stick where the frog meets the stick, Photo 27;

Photo No. 26

Photo No. 27   **Photo No. 28**   **Photo No. 29**   **Photo No. 30**

4. place the second finger over the stick opposite the thumb, so that the stick is nestled in the crease of the first joint nearest to the finger tip, Photo 28;

5. place the third finger on and over the stick, close to the second finger. The tip of the third finger should point in the direction of the pearl button on the frog. It may even cover the button, Photo 29;

6. the tip of the little finger is placed on the inner side of the top of the bow, more toward the palm of the hand, Photo 30;

7. place the first finger on the bow by curving the middle joint and over the top of the stick. For a greater margin of safety, it is best that the first finger contact the stick midway between the first and second crease. Many pupils will feel more secure if the bow is turned in the fingers so that the upper portion of the thumb nail touches the silver band of the frog. With some pupils, the thumb may touch the hair at the frog above the nail;

8. the distance between the fingers should be the same, as though the hands were hanging down naturally at the sides;

9. hold this position to the count of ten. Release the bow grip. Now hold the bow again, going through these nine steps. Do this a number of times.

Q. Are there any other effective methods of teaching a pupil to hold the bow?

A. Yes. Many teachers, working with young students, ask them to place the thumb under the frog rather than at the edge of the frog.

Another way is to hold the right arm up so that the palm of the hand faces the player. Place the bow on the fingers, so that there is a straight line from the tip of the little finger to the mid-point between the first and second knuckles of the first finger. Bend the thumb outward, so that the right side of the tip of the thumb contacts the edge of the frog opposite the second finger. Curve the fingers around the stick. Many teachers are successful presenting the bow hold in this manner.

Q. How do you teach pupils to start a bow stroke?

A. By memorizing the sensation of allowing the bow hair to form a precise contact with the string. If the first tones that the students produce are surfacy, they might play that way for quite a time.

The steps I suggest are these:
1. place the middle of the bow on the D string;
2. pinch the bow so that the hair is in firm contact with the string. This is done by an upward pressure of the thumb against the edge of the frog. The stick must be directly above the hair;
3. with the hair firmly set into the string, move the string laterally; side to side, or from right to left. The object is to do this motion without sounding the string. This will not be easy;
4. after you have done this a few times, lift the bow about six inches from the string, then replace it on the string and repeat the right to left motion. Do this on all strings;
5. now repeat this exercise midway between the middle of the bow and rip;
6. do the above exercises on two open strings at the same time.

Q. How do you teach a pupil to draw the bow for the very first time?

A. Before answering that question, I would like to say that a pupil's first experience should be a "success experience." The teacher should help the student draw the bow for the first time by holding the student's upper arm as the student draws the bow across the D string and then across the A string. The first experience should be playing quarter notes with a slight pause between the notes. We will refer to these notes as the Detaché Lancé.

The bow stroke should start from the middle and go as near as possible to the tip, depending upon the length of the pupil's arms. After a few attempts, the students should be able to do this alone.

Q. Why should there be a pause between the notes?

A. During this pause, the pupil memorizes the sensation of opening and closing the lower arm from the elbow joint.

Q. How much of the hair should be used?

A. The full width of the hair. Many of the well-known performers will use the side of the hair for artistic purposes.

Q. Should the stick be tilted toward the scroll?

A. No. The stick should be directly above the hair, but this may be considered as a variable.

Q. When will you introduce various rhythms?

A. The next experience, done with the aid of the teacher, is to play the following rhythms:

A few days later, or at the next lesson, these rhythms should be added:

Q. How long should the pupil practice above the middle of the bow?

A. I would say for a few weeks, but the teacher has to decide this. I cannot stress enough the need for creative teaching. This means that the teacher has to make many spontaneous decisions during the learning process.

Q. Before students start drawing the bow below the middle, what sensations should they memorize?

A. Pupils should feel that the entire right arm is very light and that it can float in mid-air. Hold the upper arm up, with the hand in front of the face as though playing on the D string. Push the arm lightly with the left hand and then allow the entire arm to swing to the right and back to the starting position, slowly and smoothly. The elbow should be as high as the hand itself. Do this a number of times. (♩ = M.M. 60)

The next exercise is to bring the right arm high over the right shoulder so that the finger tips touch the shoulder blade, as far over as possible. Photo 31.

Bring the arm down slowly as though you are stretching a spring that is attached to the shoulder blade. Photo 32.

Photo No. 31

Photo No. 32

You will now memorize the sensation of withholding some of the bow weight from the string.

Q. How would you divide the practice time between the lower and upper half of the bow?

A. In various ways. An entire practice period might be devoted to the upper half and another period to the lower half. An exercise might be practiced both ways; in the upper half and in the lower half.

Q. How soon would you start allowing the pupil to use the full length of the bow?

A. At the discretion of the teacher. It may be a or two or longer. I ask the pupil to place a mark week in the middle of the bow. A chalk mark or piece of adhesive tape will do. Remember the following, which is approximate.

Below the middle of the bow, the side of the hair is to be used with the stick slightly tilted toward the scroll. Above the middle of the bow, use the full width of the hair with the stick directly above the hair. When you play fortissimo you may start with the full width of the hair, even before reaching the middle.

For pianissimo, you may use the side of the hair, even after passing the middle. When you play fortissimo, above the middle, the first finger on the bow may be separated from the other three fingers slightly for better leverage.

For beginners, you might adopt the exercise of changing from side to flat at the middle of the bow. As a preliminary exercise you might adopt this approach: play a D-major scale in whole bows; at the third beat of each measure the teacher will say, "Change!"; at that moment, on the down bow, the pupil will go from side to flat; on the up-bow the pupil will go from flat to side.

Q. At the frog, how high should the elbow be?

A. It should be as high as the top of the hand and as high as the middle knuckle of the first finger.

Q. There are many players, however, who slightly lower the elbow when playing at the frog. Do you approve of this?

A. Yes, as long as it is not lower than the tip of the thumb when playing at the frog.

Q. Which is preferable?

A. I favor the height of the elbow in a straight line with the top of the hand at the frog.

Q. How high should the elbow be when playing at the middle of the bow?

A. When playing at the middle of the bow, the upper and lower arm, bow, and fingerboard should form a square. The first finger, hand, and lower arm should be parallel to the floor.

Q. Is this square always in the middle of the bow?

A. No. It depends on the length of the arm. It may be slightly above or below the middle.

Q. We know that at the frog of the bow, the little finger is to be curved to the fullest extent, with only the tip resting on the stick. How should the fingers be placed when arriving at the tip or near the tip?

A. The fingers are somewhat straightened, but in a relaxed manner.

Q. How can we tell if the fingers are straightened properly at the tip?

A. A simple way to determine this is while holding the bow properly to allow the tip of the bow to touch the tip of the chin. When you examine your fingers, you will have a fairly good idea of how the fingers should feel and look.

Q. How high should the wrist be when playing at the tip of the bow?

A. The height of the wrist might be at the same level with the tip of the thumb. It should not be drastically sunken in.

Q. How high should the wrist be when playing at the tip of the bow?

A. The height of the wrist might be at the same level with the tip of the thumb. It should not be drastically sunken in.

Q. What suggestions have you to help memorize the sensation of string levels?

A. Practice exercises similar to four-string arpeggios:

Practice these in separate bows, two to a bow, and four to a bow. The object is to go smoothly from one string to another. The bow is drawn in a vertical curve, rather than in a straight line. The right elbow should always be as high as the bow stick on each string.

On the E string the elbow should be about three or four inches from the side of the body. For most players, when playing on the lowest string, the elbow should be about the same height as the shoulder.

For additional bow control and smooth string connections, continue with the next exercise, practicing it in the following ways:

1. starting down bow in the upper half of the bow;
2. starting up bow in the lower half of the bow;
3. with the hand and fingers (about two inches of bow)
   a. at the frog,
   b. at the middle,
   c. at the tip.

Q. What are the different ways to start a bow stroke?

A. There are three basic ways to start a bow stroke:

1. the bow is on the string before starting the stroke smoothly;
2. the bow is on the string, but is started with a martelé accent;
3. the bow is in motion above the string before it touches the string.

The first way is to start a tone with the bow already on the string. The tone begins without any accent; it is a stroke that starts smoothly. The bow may be drawn slowly or quickly at the start of the stroke, depending on whether it is to be played piano or forte.

Q. Have you an exercise to help develop such a smooth start?

A. Yes. Place the bow about a half inch above the string. Let us assume it is the D string and at the frog. Make sure there is a straight line between the elbow and the tip of the thumb. With the hand in this position, lower the bow to the string by straightening the fingers. ONLY THE FINGERS. This assumes, of course, that when the bow is above the string, the little finger is curved and the thumb is curved outward. When the bow is lowered onto the string with the use of the fingers, they straighten out slightly.

Q. What is the second way of starting a bow stroke?

A. The second way is with a martelé accent. The bow is pinched with an upward pressure of the thumb against the frog, as though pressing a button. The bow hair is then set into the string, resting on the string before the stroke is begun. Most of the bow pressure is released simultaneously with the drawing of the bow. This is called the MARTELÉ ACCENT. With the lower string instruments much less pressure is released.

This bow stroke with the martelé accent may be started in forte or piano, but the important thing to remember is that it starts with the bow set into the string before it is drawn.

Q. What exercise do you have to help develop the skill of starting a stroke in this manner?

A. In the following exercise I would like the pupil to memorize the sensation of allowing the hair of the bow to sink into the string.

Place the frog of the bow on the lowest string. Pinch the bow so that the side of the hair is pressed firmly into the string with the stick tilted slightly toward the scroll. With the hair pressed firmly into the string, move the string laterally a few times, without creating a sound.

Q. How would you start the third way — with the bow in motion above the string?

A. Create a small circle near the frog and above the string. At the bottom of the circle the bow glides gently onto the string starting the bow stroke.

Starting the stroke in these three ways may be done with the vibrato at the moment the bow is drawn, or the vibrato may be started before the bow is drawn.

Q. What is the best way to start a harmonic?

A. If the harmonic is played up-bow, the bow must be on the string before playing. However, if the harmonic is played down-bow, the bow must drop lightly onto the string.

Q. What is the sensation that the player must feel in order to avoid surfacy playing?

A. There must be a communion between the hair and the string itself. The sensation to experience is one of adhesion to the string.

Q. Even in very soft playing?

A. Yes. A feeling of merely floating on the top of the string should be avoided even in pianissimo.

There are two additional sensations that every player must experience. The first is called sensation of a CENTER BALANCE in the bow hold.

Q. How can the sensation of center balance be memorized?

A. By holding the bow with the thumb and two middle fingers.

Q. What practical value is there in experiencing this sensation?

A. Many of our bowings can be more successfully performed with an emphasis on this center balance.

Q. What is a practical way to apply this to elementary students?

A. A simple, effective exercise is to have students play a D major scale in quarter notes in the upper part of the bow, starting from one to two inches below the middle. It is advisable to have the students repeat each note several times. The bow is to be held with only the *thumb and the two middle fingers*.

Q. For this exercise do you still insist on using the full width of the hair?

A. Yes. For violins and violas, the full width of the hair is to be used, with the stick directly above the hair. However, many fine players use the side of the hair. Be sure that the students draw their bows by opening and closing the lower arm from the elbow joint.

Q. What is the second sensation necessary to avoid playing with a surfacy sound?

A. The second sensation is the LEVERAGE BALANCE.

Q. How does the player memorize the sansation of a leverage balance?

A. When the bow is held with the thumb, first finger and little finger. Here is the thumb serves as a fulcrum, and the sensation is one of see-sawing between the first and fourth fingers. The tip of the little finger is in contact with the top of the stick.

I point out that I prefer the little finger to be placed on the stick not at the very top, but more toward the palm of the hand. Since the stick is usually octagon shaped at the frog, it should not be difficult to place the little finger properly.

Q. Why do you ask it to be held nearer to the palm of the hand than at the very top of the stick?

A. It is likely to provide a bit more control as the bow approaches the tip.

Q. Do you allow the tip of the little finger to leave the stick at the tip?

A. I would prefer it to remain on the stick if the shape of the hand and the length of the arm permit it. There is a slight advantage in allowing the little finger to remain on the stick.

Q. Let us return to the concept of the "leverage balance." What sort of exercise would you suggest for this?

A. The elementary student will play a D major scale above the middle of the bow in quarter notes, each note four times. The bow is to be held with only the thumb, first and fourth fingers. Pieces may also be played in this manner.

These should also be practiced below the middle of the bow. The purpose is to make sure that the pupils realize how important the first and fourth fingers are in developing a good bow arm.

To develop good bow discipline I suggest that pupils memorize the sensation of using the *entire upper half* of the bow and the *entire lower half,* while not lessening the bow length by even half an inch.

Q. What bowings clearly demonstrate the role of the first and fourth fingers?

A. The varieties of the detaché, martelé, staccato, and spiccato bowings are good examples. When playing above the middle of the bow, the weight of the arm is transferred to the first finger. However, below the middle of the bow, the weight of the arm falls on the little finger.

Q. When do you introduce the various points of contact with the bow between the bridge and the fingerboard?

A. As early as possible — possibly within the first few months of study. It means telling the pupil that the bow can be drawn in five different places between the fingerboard and the bridge. I call these the five LANES.

Q. If a pupil cannot draw a straight bow in one lane, why would you introduce five lanes where the bow can be drawn?

A. When a pupil fails to draw a straight bow in one lane, the introduction of five lanes, for some reason, makes the pupil more conscious of a straight bow.

Q. Where are the five different lanes?

A. 1. *at the fingerboard,* but not on it;
  2. *near the fingerboard,* midway between the center and the fingerboard;
  3. *at the center,* midway between the bridge and the fingerboard;

4. *near the bridge*, midway between the center and the bridge;

5. *at the bridge*, as close as possible to the bridge without touching it.

Q. How would you introduce the five lanes?

A. First, the pupils should develop a kinesthetic sense of the various distances between the fingerboard and the bridge.

I suggest the following exercise. *Drop* the bow on the D string two or three inches above the middle of the bow. Do this in quarter notes in the first lane. Allow the bow to drop vertically and silently like the bouncing of a rubber ball from a height of about two inches from the string. This vertical bouncing should be done, if possible, with a see-saw motion involving the index finger and the little finger.

While the tone will be practically silent, play a D-major scale, each note four times. The scale should again be played in each of the five lanes.

For another interesting effect in classroom teaching, ask half of the class to play the scale using the detaché bowing on the string and the other half to play it with the bouncing strokes. Then reverse the groups.

Q. Why do we use less hair as we approach the frog, particularly on the violin?

A. We remove the inner edge of the hair from the string to compensate for the natural increase in the weight of the bow. If we use the full width of the hair at the frog, too much of the surface of the string is covered, which could possibly prevent a free vibration of the string.

It also helps to preserve a straight bow a little more readily. Another reason is that it can be helpful in developing a slight bending of the wrist at the frog. It also contributes to the flexibility of the hand in the wrist joint.

Many teachers ask their pupils to use the full width of the hair, even at the frog, for the sake of additional bow discipline. There is much justification for this on an advanced level, particularly on the lower strings.

Q. How do we develop a relaxed bow arm?

A. Before I answer that, I would like to say that a number of years ago I consulted an orthopedist, a psychologist, a psychiatrist, and a very learned educator. They were unanimous about the word "relaxed." They felt that the use of the word "relaxed" might not be suitable because very little can be done with a relaxed bow arm. When we attempt any motion, there must be some contraction. What we wish to achieve is a working arm in which the various parts of the arm coordinate, in a manner that will bring about freedom of activity and freedom of motion.

Q. How would you define freedom of motion?

A. Freedom of motion is when the hand in the wrist joint, the lower arm in the elbow joint, and the entire upper arm, starting from the shoulder joint, work together in a flexible manner. They must move as if operated on hinges so that the motion will require a minimum of effort. Their action must be well coordinated so that one part can assume an active role, while the others assume a passive role.

For some bowings we will want an action of the hand in the wrist joint. For others, we may want an active action of the lower arm, starting from the elbow joint, with a passive action of the upper arm.

Q. Do you have a basic exercise that will be helpful to achieve freedom of motion in the right arm?

A. There is a series of them to be done without the bow, but if you ask for the most important sensation which the pupils must experience, I would like to suggest this one: the sensation is that of being able to imagine a whip, and that the upper arm is the stick of the whip, while the lower arm and hand represent the whip itself. By moving the entire arm up and down as if snapping a whip with a very flexible hand in the wrist joint, one experiences that freedom of motion. The sensation is that of strength in the entire arm, but with great freedom of motion in the various joints.

Here are four additional basic exercises. The first one is as follows: extend your right arm all the way in front of the shoulder. Raise it above your head and come down in a wavy motion, as though describing a wave in the ocean.

The outstretched arm and hand should be level with the shoulder and should feel as if suspended by a flexible cord in the back muscles. The wrist should feel very light as it moves up and down from the height of the shoulder upward to the point where the middle joint of each finger faces the ceiling. The hand in the wrist joint, the elbow joint and the shoulder joint should feel very flexible and free.

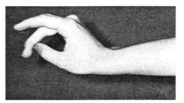

Photo No. 33

Here is the second basic exercise for achieving freedom of motion in the right arm. Raise the right arm so that the hand is in front of the nose. The elbow should be as high as though playing at the frog on the D string. In this position, create a circle with the entire arm moving freely. The complete circle should go a bit over the head and come back so that the hand is always in front of the nose. Do this at least six times, clockwise, as though playing up-bow. Pause for a moment with the hand in front of the nose and then do it counter-clockwise.

The third exercise will also help to memorize the sensation of lightness and freedom of motion in the entire arm. Hold the right arm up again in the same position as in the second exercise, with the elbow as high as the shoulder. With the left hand gently push the arm slightly to the right. Now allow the arm, from the shoulder joint, to move from right to left. Try to memorize the sensation of the arm never stopping.

When the arm is moved to the right, it should move as far to the right as though reaching the tip of the bow. There should be an obtuse angle between the upper and lower arm when the arm is at or close to the tip. When the arm is drawn up-bow and the hand is in front of the face, there should be an acute angle between the upper and lower arm.

The fourth exercise for freedom of motion in the right arm is also done without holding the bow. Place the tip of the right thumb in the first joint of the middle finger, the joint nearest the tip of the finger. The elbow should be on the same level as the shoulder. Create a large circle starting from the shoulder joint, the entire arm moving lightly and freely as though starting down-bow. Do this at least six times.

Now create the same circle as though starting up-bow. Try to experience the sensation of the arm being airborne.

Now create a circle much smaller, because we want the action to stem from the elbow joint. In other words, one must memorize the sensation of opening and closing the elbow as this circle is created in the air. The upper arm must remain quiet. This might be a little more difficult because there are two simultaneous sensations: (1) the freedom of motion in the shoulder joint, and (2) the freedom of motion in the elbow joint as it open and closes.

Next, we create circles that are smaller because we want the action to stem from the hand in the wrist joint. In other words, create small circles, clockwise and counter clockwise, with just the hand and a passive action of the lower arm. Do this a number of times.

When we create the large circles from the shoulder joint, the entire arm must be free, with practically no motion from the elbow or wrist joints. When we create the smaller circles where the action comes from the elbow joint, there will be some passive action in the upper arm, and very little, if any, from the hand. When we create the very small circles from the hand in the wrist joint, there should be some inward turning of the lower arm in the elbow joint, but we must try to keep the upper arm as quiet as possible.

Q. What suggestions have you to avoid or eliminate the raising or hunching of the right shoulder as some players approach the frog?

A. Make sure that the tip of the right elbow is at the same height as the top (back) of the hand. Avoid tension in the entire arm. The student must concentrate on a well-lubricated shoulder joint and freedom of motion. Gripping the bow too tightly when playing forte is frequently responsible for tension and should be avoided.

Q. Do you incorporate breathing in connection with these exercises to develop freedom of motion?

A. Yes. Here is an exercise where we attempt to accomplish it: play a D-major scale in half notes, using the entire bow. After each stroke introduce a half rest. Lift the bow high above the head during the rest, and bring the bow down in the form of a circle for the next note. Start each note with the weight of the body on the left foot. For the second beat of the half note, transfer the entire weight of the body to the right foot in a swaying motion. During the half rest, as the bow is being brought up in a circle, transfer the weight to the left foot, ready to start the next note. Take a deep breath during the half rest.

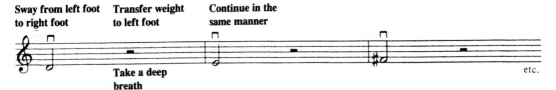

Sway from left foot to right foot   Transfer weight to left foot   Continue in the same manner

Take a deep breath

Q. How do we go from one bow to another smoothly, particularly at the frog?

A. That is not easy to describe. Some pupils seem to develop this skill quite naturally, while others have to practice for a length of time to achieve it. It is, however, essential that all pupils develop a smooth bow change in all parts of the bow. At the frog, the actual change of the bow is made by an up-bow movement of the fingers about a half inch, while the entire arm is already starting the down-bow stroke. During this motion, the thumb gradually straigthens. This will mean a very subtle transferring of the weight of the bow hand from the top of the stick to the side nearest the bridge. In doing this, the stick might tilt slightly toward the scroll. The little finger rests on the top of the stick more toward the inner side, toward the palm, and must remain curved to the fullest extent. The little finger is to be curved when the thumb straightens out. It is advisable to watch the palm of the hand. You will find that the center of the palm during the bow change will be in a parallel line with the frog. Advanced players should develop a bow change that is done with only the fingers when playing piano or pianissimo. If the volume is greater, the bow change might be made with the hand and fingers.

In forte or fortissimo, the change can be made with the lower arm with flexible hand and fingers. During the bow change we must avoid a jerky sound.

We might put it another way. We must avoid accenting the note as we change the bow. There is a natural tendency to speed up the bow before the change is made. The bow should slow down a bit before the bow change. There should also be a slight lessening of the weight of the bow on the string during the bow change at the frog. The real test is when the bow change is smoothly made without an actual loss of volume. It requires a well-coordinated freedom of motion between the upper arm, lower arm, and the hand and fingers.

Q. When would you start teaching this smooth bow change?

A. As soon as a pupil is able to do a hand and finger stroke (a small detaché that involves just the hand and fingers). You could start in the first year. This is the way I would present it to a pupil.

"Place the middle of the bow on the D string. Draw the bow slowly toward the frog, up-bow. Stop the bow as soon as you get to about two inches from the frog. Complete the bow stroke, using only the hand and fingers, while the upper and lower arm remain quiet. Stop when you get to the frog. Your thumb and first finger should be somewhat straighened, but your little finger must be curved. Now examine your hand. The center of the palm of the hand should be parallel to the frog.

"Now start playing down-bow, with the entire arm initiating the down-bow movement. After some practice you will eliminate the stop at the frog, so that the hand and fingers will complete the up-bow stroke simultaneously with the entire arm intitiating the down-bow."

Q. How do I develop a smooth bow change at the tip?

A. Draw the bow to about one or two inches from the tip. Lower the hand slightly in the wrist joint as though changing to the next higher string without actually touching it.

Start the up-bow stroke with the entire arm at the same instant that you lower the hand. If the bow change is smooth, the bow should create an action that is similar to that of the tail of a fish as it swims. The feeling might also be that you are creating a slight circle.

Q. How can one avoid the trembling of the bow when playing long notes that are played softly?

A. One of the manifestations of nervousness is a trembling of the bow, particularly around the middle. It is important that you attempt to determine the cause. This lack of bow control may be the result of insufficient bow technic, or it could be just mental. Much of the difficulty can be avoided by practicing the hand and finger stroke in different parts of the bow: at the frog, six inches from the frog, in the middle, six inches from the tip, and at the tip.

Sometimes the difficulty might be traced to holding the bow too tightly or even too loosely. The player must examine the bow grip. Trembling may frequently be eliminated by making sure there is a slight, inward turning of the lower arm in the elbow joint in a rotary motion when playing around the middle of the bow. When experimenting with the bow hold, try to apply a bit more upward pressure of the thumb against the frog. Sometimes the trembling can be elminated by lightening the pressure of the two middle fingers on the bow stick. It may be helpful to practice slow whole bows in whole and half notes with the two middle fingers removed from the bow stick.

Faulty breathing or lack of breathing should be carefully considered.

Try using a little less hair throughout the entire bow stroke. In order to do that, however, you may have to slightly tighten the bow hair, and, while I am not particularly happy about doing this, it may be worthwhile if it avoids the trembling.

In public performance, it may be better to change bows more frequently in order to avoid long sustained tones. Many fine players do just that.

Q. How would you describe the different ways to produce accents?

A. Accents are created in three possible ways:
1. by a quickening of the bow, using more bow length at the beginning of the stroke;
2. by applying more weight on the string at the start of the note;
3. by a combination of the two.

In piano or pianissimo, we might create the accents at the beginning of the note by just a slight quickening of the bow. In forte or fortissimo apply additional bow weight and speed. Actually, much of our playing depends upon the application of accents. We must study the way we produce accents, making sure that we use the correct bow lane as well as the appropriate speed and pressure. The life blood of playing, describing different emotions, is related to accents and the way we produce them.

Q. When we have a series of notes which we wish to accent, for example, a series of quarter notes, and we want to accent each note, do we leave a pause between the notes?

A. That depends on whether we are using the martelé or detaché bowings. With the martelé bowing, there is to be a clean stop between the accented notes. The tone is to be continuous when we produce accents using the detaché bowing.

Q. Is the left hand helpful in producing accents?

A. Yes, it can be particularly helpful in shifts. We can create a slight accent by striking the note with the left hand a bit more forcefully. We might refer to this as a FINGER ACCENT.

Q. How much louder should the accented note be than the note before it?

A. The best way to answer that is to regard each dynamic mark as being bound by an orbit or range of volume. The additional volume on each accented note must be guided by good musical taste. At no time should this additional volume go beyond the orbit of the dynamic mark.

For example, when playing "piano," the note or notes that are accented are to remain in the "piano" orbit. The dynamic range of the orbit varies according to the size and acoustics of the room or auditorium.

Q. Is there an additional way that we can measure the range of the various orbits?

A. You can do the following: regard each orbit as having a numerical range of one through five. If the dynamic range is "forte," the basic volume will be "one." Each higher number will mean a slight additional volume, so that number "five" will still be within the orbit of the "forte."

In duet playing the accompanying part will be played number one, while the melody will be played in the additional volume of number two through five. Both parts, however, will remain in the "forte" orbit.

Q. When changing bows at the frog, some players have a tendency to accent the note so that the volume will sound beyond the dynamic orbit. How can this be avoided?

A. By slowing the speed of the bow as the frog is approached.

Q. How can players be sure that they are drawing a straight bow that is parallel to the bridge? What suggestions do you have to offer?

A. I would say to the students, "Place the bow on the D string at the frog. Draw the bow slowly for eight beats (circa ♩ + 72)."

From the frog to near the middle, you must feel that you are pulling the bow with the entire arm. When you arrive at the middle or slightly below the middle, the feeling of pulling the bow must lessen. Otherwise the bow might leave the lane, or the tip of the bow might slide down toward the fingerboard.

From the middle to the tip, the sensation you must experience is that of pushing the frog slightly away from the body. This will help insure a straight bow.

Q. How would you describe the up-bow?

A. On the up-bow the sensation is that of pulling the bow. As you get nearer the middle, the sensation is that of pushing the bow to the frog, which is to be brought a bit closer to the body.

Q. Suppose the pupil cannot memorize the sensation of opening and closing the elbow when playing above the middle of the bow? What suggestions can you offer?

A. The students should play open strings in the upper half of the bow with the tip of the right elbow touching a wall. This should be followed by playing scales in the upper half with the pupils looking at and concentrating on the right elbow.

Q. How does one develop the feeling of a balanced bow hold?

A. Here are three exercises:
1. Without the violin, hold the bow in playing position with the hair parallel to the floor; lift and replace the first finger on the stick sixteen times in slow quarter notes; do the same with the second, third, and fourth finger;
2. This exercise develops the feeling of a center of balance; this is acquired by being able to hold the bow in playing position with the first finger, little finger, and thumb; lift and replace the second and third fingers simultaneously on the stick; do this sixteen times;
3. Hold the bow parallel to the floor; remove the first, second and third fingers from the bow — this means that only the thumb and little finger will be holding the bow; try to balance and maintain the bow hold for eight counts with only the thumb and little finger.

Q. How do we develop flexibility of the fingers of the right hand?

A. Hold the bow with the tip of the bow pointing toward the ceiling. Crawl with the fingers up an down the entire stick without touching the hair. Do this quite slowly. Take a deep breath when at the frog, at the middle, and at the tip of the bow. Keep the thumb and middle fingers opposite each other without moving the arm. The arm should be as motionless as possible during this crawling exercise.

Now repeat the same exercise, holding the bow parallel to the floor.

Q. What is one way to memorize the sensation of transferring the weight of the arm to the first finger on the bow?

A. Hold the bow six inches from the frog. In this bow position, play a scale in quarter notes, each note four times, using the entire upper half of the bow. Use the full width of the bow hair with the stick directly above the hair. Now repeat this same scale, holding the bow stick in the middle of the bow.

The Specific Bowings and How to Teach Them

Q. How would you define the DÉTACHÉ bowing?

A. The détaché is a smooth stroke played in separate bows and in any part of the bow. There is to be a continuous sound between the down-bow and the up-bow strokes. The détaché bowing must not be confused with the word "detached." It does not mean, as some players assume, cleanly articulated and separated strokes.

Q. How much of the hand or arm is used in this bowing?

A. For the détaché you may use:
1. the hand, or wrist;
2. the hand in conjunction with the lower arm, where most of the activity starts from the elbow joint;
3. the lower arm in conjunction with the upper arm, depending on the length of the stroke.

I would like to make it clear that when we concentrate on the hand, there is bound to be some passive action of the lower arm. When we use the lower arm, there is bound to be some passive action of the upper arm.

Q. What are some practical suggestions for developing a good détaché in the upper half of the bow?

A. Many players use the full width of the hair, with the stick directly above the hair. The bow must at all times be parallel to the bridge and a bit nearer to the fingerboard than to the bridge when playing in the lower positions.

Concentrate on an active use of the lower arm by opening and closing the elbow joint. The upper arm becomes active only when we go from one string to another. Avoid a "surfacy" sound by making sure that the bow hair clings firmly to the string. Listen carefully to make sure that the up-bow sound is as firm as the down-bow sound. A good idea is to practice détaché etudes starting up-bow. When playing at or near the tip of the bow, the top of the wrist should be practically at a level with the tip of the thumb. There must be an inward turning of the forearm as the tip is approached. One is likely to get a firmer sound if the base knuckles are at the side of the stick and somewhat parallel to the stick. As we approach the tip, there must be a feeling of the bow being drawn away from the body, and on the up-bow, as being drawn closer to the body.

Q. What about the little finger when we play above the middle of the bow?

A. It is best for the little finger to remain on the stick. However, many fine players remove the little finger from the bow. Those players who have very short fourth fingers have two choices. The first choice is to remove the fourth finger as the tip is approached. The second choice, and this is the better one, is to keep the little finger on the stick, but just avoid getting all the way to the tip of the bow. It is often not possible for many young players to use the last one or two inches of the bow at the tip.

Q. Is that because, with many young players, the bow is often longer than the pupil's arm?

A. Yes. If they use the entire length of the bow, they cannot draw it parallel to the bridge all the way to the tip.

Q. When we refer to an unusually fine détaché above the middle of the bow, just what is meant?

A. We mean the ability to play a détaché stroke starting about three or four inches below the middle of the bow and getting to the tip and back without an active use of the upper arm.

Q. If we start the détaché from the middle, we form a square, but when we start a few inches below the middle, would that not form an acute angle between the upper and lower arm?

A. Yes. That would be starting at an acute angle. At the tip it would be an obtuse angle. The important thing to remember is that only the lower arm is to be used. If the upper arm is brought into play, it should be only when going from one string to another.

Q. When you start below the middle of the bow would you still use the full width of the hair from acute to obtuse?

A. Yes. However, if we start below the middle at a dynamic level of pianissimo, we might start with the side of the hair and gradually use more hair as we approach the tip.

I like to refer to this as an unusually fine détaché stroke, which means being able to play with ease from acute to obtuse. I sometimes also call this the GREATER UPPER-HALF DÉTACHÉ. It is not enough just be able to play from middle to tip. The ability to play a détaché in the middle third of the bow without an active use of the upper arm is extremely desirable.

Q. What comment would you make if we wish to play the détaché rapidly?

A. When we speed up the détaché we must bear in mind one thing, and that is that we gradually move away from the tip and closer to the middle. A rapid détaché too near the tip is likely to produce a "surfacy" sound.

Q. But suppose we are to play an extremely rapid détaché?

A. It then becomes a hand and finger, smooth détaché stroke around the middle of the bow.

Q. What comments would you make on performing the détaché in the lower half of the bow?

A. Here the sensation should be of an upper arm that can move with great freedom. The whole arm must feel very light and as though it is well lubricated at the shoulder joint. We must get the feeling that we can play swiftly and lightly from the frog to the middle.

What actually happens is that when we use the upper arm, the whole arm moves downward and a bit backward. At the frog the elbow should be on the same level as the hand. If we play fortissimo, we might use the full width of the hair. In piano or pianissimo, we might use less hair with the stick tilted slightly toward the scroll.

As we approach the frog on the up-bow, we must make sure that the left side of the hand is always at right angles to the stick.

Q. How can we become equally proficient in playing at the frog and at the tip?

A. By playing exercises which will involve playing four eighth notes in the lower part of the bow near the frog. This may be followed by a half note which will take us all the way to the tip. The next four eighth notes should then be played at the tip and again, using a whole bow, to get back to the frog. Extend this exercise by starting with notes in the upper third and lower third of the bow, the upper and lower fourth, then the upper or lower half, always a whole bow in between.

For the advanced player, many of the bowing studies in the book, The Best of Sevcik, Vol. 2, have to be played at the frog, middle and tip.

For elementary students in their first or second year of study, I would like to recommend the bowing exercises in the book, Etudes for Technic and Musicianship, Vols. 2 and 3.

There are times when a pupil should devote a 15-minute period to etudes that are to be played in the upper half of the bow, and then another period of time concentrating on the lower half of the bow. For very advanced players there are a number of studies by Kreutzer, Fiorillo, Rodé that will provide good material.

Another good idea is to take a détaché etude (and this may be done at all levels of advancement), playing each measure twice. Play the first measure twice in the first quarter of the bow and, without stopping, play the next measure twice in the second quarter of the bow, third measure in the third quarter, and the fourth measure in the fourth quarter of the bow.

The same thing can be done using the lower third of the bow, then the middle third of the bow, then the upper third of the bow. Continue in the same manner, working your way back to the frog.

Q. What is your definition of the SMALL DETACHÉ?

A. A SMALL DETACHÉ is a smooth stroke in separate bows that involves only two or three inches of bow. The hand from the wrist joint is used, with the fingers always remaining flexible.

Q. When is this hand-finger stroke (the wrist stroke) used?

A. Most of the time when playing piano or pianissimo with eighth or sixteenth notes. We might use this stroke even in mezzo-forte. It may be played rapidly or slowly.

Q. When should this bowing be introduced to the student?

A. As soon as possible during the first year of study.

Q. How would you teach this hand and finger stroke?

A. I would first present some preliminary exercises without the violin or bow to help memorize the sensation of freedom of motion of the hand in the wrist joint. This would also include flexiblity of the fingers.

The first exercise is as follows: hold a pencil in three basic positions. In the first two of these positions the elbow should at all times be as high as the top of the hand. The first basic position is with the hand held in front of the face as though the bow is at the frog. The upper and lower arm form an acute angle.

In the second basic position hold the arm as though playing in the middle of the bow. The lower arm, the upper arm, the bow and the neck of the instrument form a square.

In the third basic position move the lower arm to form an obtuse angle as though playing near the tip of the bow. In the third basic position the top of the hand will be a little lower than the elbow joint. In these three basic positions move the hand in the wrist joint up and down in quarter notes and eighth notes. Then create a complete circle with the hand in the wrist joint, first clockwise and then counter clockwise. The important thing to concentrate on is freedom of motion in the wrist joint.

Q. What exercises do you suggest for developing the hand and finger stroke using the bow and the instrument?

A. Hold the bow about two inches above the D string. Using just the hand and fingers, draw the bow in the direction of the up-bow and the down-bow. Draw the down-bow with the fingers going from curved to straight, and the up-bow with the fingers going from straight to curved.

If you are successful with this, lower the bow to about one inch above the string. Then do the same to about ½ inch above the string. Finally, in pianissimo, allow the bow to come in contact with the D string.

This exercise should be practiced in five places; the frog; six inches from the frog, using the side of the hair with the stick tilted slightly toward the scroll; in the middle, practicing it with the side of the hair; with the flat of the hair six inches from tip; and finally, at the tip. These should be done in quarter notes, and then in eighth notes.

Q. Suppose a pupil finds it difficult using just the hand and fingers from the wrist joint?

A. Then do it again slowly in the following manner. This is how I would explain it to a pupil:

"Place the bow on the D string about six inches from the frog. Use this side of the hair. Make sure that your elbow is as high as the top of the hand. Now, curve your fingers. Draw the bow down-bow about two inches, using only the wrist and fingers. Try it a few times. If you cannot do it, I am going to hold your lower arm and have to do it a few times so that you can memorize the sensation of moving just the hand. Do it only down-bow for a few times. Now, let's see if you can do it without my holding your arm.

"Now, let's try it going back up-bow. Notice that as you went down-bow, the fingers straightened out. Stop after each note. Now, here we are. You played it down-bow, for two inches, and you stopped. Your fingers are now somewhat straightened. Try to go back up two inches, but as you do, curve your fingers. I am going to hold your lower arm again so that you can move freely from down-bow to up-bow. Do this exercise many times."

Continue holding the lower arm until the pupil is able to develop freedom of the hand in the wrist joint. You might also try placing the pupil's lower arm at the top of a chair or sofa for a while.

Q. Suppose a pupil finds it difficult to develop flexible fingers. What do we do then?

A. You will say to the pupil, "Hold a small eraser in the finger tips of your right hand. Make believe you are erasing something. This will help you memorize the sensation of using just the fingers.

"On a piece of paper draw a few vertical lines about one inch long. Take an eraser. Hold it between the thumb and first two fingers. Place the hand on the sheet of paper and erase these lines, using only the fingers.

"Now, draw a series of horizontal lines about one inch long. Place your hand on the paper in a slanting position as though playing up-bow and down-bow. Now, erase these lines, using only the fingers and hand. This will be the manner in which the hand and fingers move in the performance of the small détaché."

After this we will apply three well-known exercises for finger flexing. Here they are:
1. hold the bow in an upright position so that the tip of the bow points to the ceiling; with the hand hold the right hand at the wrist joint. In this position the pupil will possibly be able to move the bow so that the point comes closer to the ceiling; the fingers will curve and then straighten out as the pupil lower the bow; (do this in quarter notes and eighth notes);
2. when the pupil is successful in doing this, turn the bow so that the hair and the palm of the hand the ceiling. Now, while the left hand is still holding the right wrist move the bow using only the fingers, from right to left;
3. the third way is the most difficult. Turn the bow so that the hair faces the floor as though playing the instrument. While still holding the hand at the wrist move the bow from right to left, using only the fingers. This is the most difficult because the bow seems heaviest in this position. This is a long term achievement. We must not permit the pupil to become discouraged.

Q. Should the sensation be in the wrist joint or in the fingertips?

A. If you imagine that the action is concentrated in the fingertips, you are more likely to get the correct type of finger activity that coordinates with the hand in the wrist joint. If you concentrate only on the feeling in the wrist joint, the fingers might not be flexible enough. However, this may vary with different pupils.

Q. What about the elbow when we use this hand-finger stroke?

A. The elbow should always be on the same level of the string being played.

Q. What is your definition of the GRAND DÉTACHÉ?

A. It is a whole bow détaché with a continuous sound between the down-bow and the up-bow. We start at the frog, using the side of the hair with the fingers curved. As we approach the middle of the bow, we gradually use the full width of the hair. Remember that on the down-bow as we approach the middle, the upper arm goes down slightly and backwards. From near the middle, the lower arm continues the stroke to the very tip. At the tip the fingers on the bow straighten out somewhat. The important things is to make sure that the bow is always parallel to the bridge thorughout the entire bow stroke and that the volume at the tip must be just as strong as at the frog.

Q. How would you describe the performance of the ACCENTED GRAND DÉTACHÉ?

A. In this bowing we must make sure that the accent is created by a quicker drawing of the bow at the start of the stroke, slowing down as we proceed to the end of the bow.

Q. Doesn't this present the problem of adjusting to the proper lane?

A. Yes, it does. When we draw the bow quickly we must be at lower lane, near the fingerboard. When we slacken the bow speed we must move closer to the bridge, but when we draw fast whole bows we haven't much time to adjust the lane.

The quickening of the bow at the start of the stroke and the slowing down of the bow towards the end of the stroke requires considerable experience. It would be well to spend a good deal of time practicing the ACCENTED GRAND DÉTACHÉ.

When we use the GRAND DÉTACHÉ, it is usually in a manner that is majestic, requiring breadth of style. A subtle sensation that may be helpful is to draw the down-bow on the lowest level of the same string; i.e. closer to the next higher string. On the up-bow we draw the bow on the highest level, closer to the next lower string.

Q. So you mean that the arm level is changed?

A. Yes, but only very slightly. The feeling of higher or lower is very slight. We must experience the sensation of pulling the tone from the instrument. Too many players try to force the tone out.

Q. How would you describe the sensation of pulling the tone out and not pressing it out?

A. First, remember that pressing the bow does not produce a large sound. If you are playing down-bow, try to imagine that there is a weight at the very tip of the bow and that you are going to pull the weight down-bow. When playing an up-bow, imagine that there is a weight at the frog and that you are going to pull the weight up-bow.

Q. How does a player decide when to use the DÉTACHÉ bowing?

A. As a rule it is the content of the music that will be the most important guide.

Q. Are there any specific indications for the détaché?

A. Yes. When you see dashes over a series of separated notes, you will use the détaché. However, there are differences of opinion as to the interpretation, depending also on the dynamic level of the passage.

Q. When you have a passage of notes in separate bows and an isolated note is marked with a dash, what does that mean?

A. It means that the isolated note is to stand out expressively from the others.

Q. Is the stroke for playing that particular note given a name?

A. Frequently we call it PORTÉ.

Q. Just how is that note to be played?

A. In order to make the note stand out a bit, we draw the bow slightly faster on that note. We may play that note a bit louder. We may vibrate more intensely. We may even hold it a little longer and compensate by playing the following note or notes a bit faster. We also refer to this stroke as "DÉTACHÉ PORTÉ".

Q. Are there any other forms of the détaché bowing?

A. When a note or a series of notes is marked with dots and dashes, it means to articulate each note gently. It is called the DÉTACHÉ LANCÉ. The articulation must not be as crisp as a martelé stroke. As a rule, the tones are to be played quite smoothly. That is, the sound should be continuous, with each note slightly articulated. We might even allow minute stopping between the notes if they are played in an expressive manner. That would mean that we might vibrate on each note if the tempo permits. However, we must not accent the notes despite the fact that each note is articulated.

Q. Frequently I will see a series of notes in one bow but with each note marked with a dash. What is the most common name for that?

A. That is called "PORTATO" but is also referred to as the "PARLANDO" or "talking" bow. Here we have a series of notes to be played in one bow stroke, but with each gently articulated or enunciated, and most of the time without a definite stop between the notes. This is a very interesting bowing, and is useful to achieve some variety in performance:

Meditation from "Thais"
J. Massenet

Q. When a pupil has a reasonably good détaché, what bowing would you introduce next?

A. Either the MARTELÉ or the COLLÉ. It depends on the pupil.

Q. How soon would you start a new bowing?

A. That also depends on the pupil, but I would suggest that you start as soon as possible in the first year. Let us take the COLLÉ.

Q. What is your definition of the COLLÉ bowing?

A. The COLLÉ is a short stroke that is chipped off the string. It starts with the hair set well into the string, which means that we do not throw the bow down onto the string. The hair is already well set into the string <u>before</u> the bow is set into motion.

Q. Can this be played in all parts of the bow?

A. Yes. It is not too frequently used, but its value for bow discipline is unlimited, and it should be practiced by every string player.

Q. How would you teach this bowing?

A. Place the bow on the string about two inches from the frog, making sure that the thumb and the little finger are curved and with the elbow as high as the top of the hand. The bow hair should be set firmly into the string.

Q. What is the sensation one should experience?

A. The sensation should be that of pinching the bow with an upward pressure of the tip of the thumb on the edge of the frog. This pressure of pinching should be firm or light, depending on the tempo and the volume. Release the pressure suddenly. At this instant the bow is to leave the string with the fingers straightening out in a spring-like action, in the direction of the down-bow. Before the bow left the string the fingers were curved. When the stroke is completed the fingers are somewhat straightened.

Q. How are the fingers placed on the up-bow COLLÉ?

A. The fingers are straight and as the bow leaves the string in the direction of the up-bow, the fingers become curved.

Q. When the bow leaves the string, how far does it travel?

A. I would say about two inches. That traveling is done with the bow above the string. Here we have an example of the COLLÉ bowing:

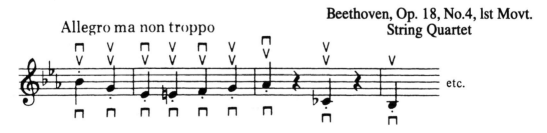

Beethoven, Op. 18, No.4, 1st Movt.
String Quartet

Practice passages similar to this in three ways:
1. all down-bows (from curved fingers to straight);
2. all up-bows (from straight fingers to curved);
3. down-bows and up-bows alternating — the collé should be practiced at the frog, six inches from the frog, in the middle, six inches from the tip, and at the tip.

In the middle and above the middle we will use the full width of the hair. It has to be practiced very slowly at the tip because it takes time to again set the hair firmly in to the string before starting the next note. Create a small circle in the air with the bow before the hair settles into the string for the next note. I also want to mention that the term "collé" is quite recent.

To develop breadth of style and bow control, practice one note with the collé at the frog, and then after a complete circle with the arm play the same note at the tip, each note down-bow. Do the same at the frog and tip, both with up-bows. Then one down-bow at the frog and one down-bow at the tip. Practice scales using the collé bowing. Elementary students may start with a one-octave scale.

Q. How would you teach the MARTELÉ bowing?

A. Place the bow on the string at the frog, with the elbow and the top of the right hand forming a straight line. Pinch the bow hair firmly into the string. Release practically all of this pressure, and at the same time draw the bow quickly but still on the string. Less pressure is released on the lower string instruments. The martelé stroke requires that there be a clean stop after each note and that each tone should start with a precise attack. At the end of the stroke the bow should not quiver during the stop.

At the frog this attack or pinching of the bow should include a slight upward pressure of the thumb. At the tip this attack is created by a slight rotary motion of the forearm, i.e. a turning of the lower arm at the elbow joint with the weight of the hand and the lower arm transferred to the first finger.

The martelé bowing is usually indicated by dots above or below each note. The martelé may be played in any part of the bow. The speed of the martelé is limited, due to the fact that there must be a clean stop after each note.

Q. What is the best part of the bow to use while playing at a fast tempo?

A. As the martelé stroke becomes more rapid, it should be played closer to the tip than to the middle.

Q. Do you refer to the GRAND MARTELÉ as the bowing that uses the entire bow, as you do with the grand détaché?

A. Yes. Here you are to use the entire bow. At the frog the fingers are curved. The bow is drawn rapidly and as the pressure is released, the fingers straighten out. Bear in mind that on the up-bow the fingers are somewhat straight at the start of the stroke and become curved when the bow is set in motion.

Q. Why is it so hard to make the up-bow attack as strong as the down-bow attack?

A. Because, it is going against the pull of gravity and so requires a lot more energy to make up for the loss of natural weight. At the beginning of each stroke, the bow should be drawn rapidly. However, it slows down toward the end of the stroke. If you are playing up-bow the upper arm must be lifted once you pass the middle, so that by the time the nut or frog is reached, the elbow and the top of the hand are practically on the same level.

The development of the GRAND MARTELÉ takes years. It should be practiced in slow quarter notes at first, with a fast drawing of the bow and a long stop after each note.

Q. How do you go from one string to another with the martelé?

A. When you cross or skip strings it is the entire arm that is brought into action. It is important to remember that you immediately go to the next string and observe the pause on the new string.

Q. What is your definition of the SPICCATO stroke?

A. A stroke in which the bow is thrown onto the string. It may be played anywhere between the frog and an inch or two above the middle of the bow.

Q. Why is it frequently called the slow or controlled spiccato bowing?

A. Because it is slower than the sautillé bowing, and because each stroke is controlled by the arm and/or hand. It can actually be played quite rapidly, but compared to the sautillé we must consider it a slow stroke.

The basis of the spiccato and the basis of the sautillé are entirely different. The basis for the spiccato is a martelé stroke, whereas the basis for the sautillé bowing is a small détaché. However, there is one similarity between them, and that is that the bow leaves the string.

Q. Why is the "spiccato" called the "artificial spiccato"?

A. I don't know. There is nothing artificial about this bowing. I think it is because we create each spiccato stroke by a motion of the hand or arm. It does not bounce by its own volition as in the sautillé stroke. It is a title we should remove entirely from the vocabulary.

Q. How high should the bow be thrown from the string?

A. That depends upon how percussive or loud you want the stroke to sound. It can vary from being very close to the string to an inch above the string.

Q. How much of the hair do you use for the spiccato bowing?

A. From very little hair with the bow stick tilted toward the scroll to most of the hair, depending on how much bow you use and how broadly you want the spiccato to sound. The emotional content of the music will have to decide that.

Q. How would you start teaching the spiccato to a pupil who has never done it before?

A. A good way is to use preparatory exercises. They are to be played for one or two weeks before the actual spiccato is taught. However, the teacher is to make the final decision as to just how long the pupil is to remain on these preparatory exercises.

Q. How would you present these preparatory exercises to the student?

A. Place the bow on the D string about four inches from the frog with all the fingers curved. Make sure that the little finger is well curved and that the middle joint of the thumb is bent outward. Draw a down-bow, using the hand and fingers for about two inches, straightening the fingers at the same time. Now draw an up-bow about two inches, curving the fingers. Use the side of the hair. It should be noted that some players, particularly violists, prefer to use the full width of the hair.

Practice in two parts of the bow:
  1. about four inches from the from;
  2. about one inch below the middle.
Play one-, two-, or three-octave scales, each note four times, using this stroke. Do this for a week or two.

Practice it on open strings in slow quarter notes. Try practicing it in double stops with two open strings played simultaneously. The tempo should be from ♩ = MM 88 to ♩ = MM 120.

Q. Assuming that the pupil has done this from one to several weeks, how do you teach the performance of the actual spiccato stroke?

A. The actual spiccato stroke is similar to the hand and finger stroke except that now the bow is to be lifted from the string instead of allowing it to remain on the string. The fingers must be very flexible. The bow is to strike the string a bit nearer to the fingerboard than to the bridge. In the very high positions the bow will strike the string closer to the bridge.

Q. Is the spiccato stroke always marked with dots above or below the note?

A. Most of the time it is, and you have to determine whether to play martelé or to use the spiccato bowing. That depends on the tempo and the volume.

Q. You refer to different styles of spiccato. Which style would you teach first?

A. I teach a heavy spiccato which I have named the DRAMATIC SPICCATO. Students seem to like this title, and it is rather descriptive. It is played at the frog with the entire arm. There is, however, a passive action of the lower arm and the hand, but the primary action is in the entire arm from the shoulder joint. It is important that the bow strike the string parallel to the bridge or at right angles to the string. The arm motion might be compared to a slight arc, with the lowest portion of the arc striking the string:

Q. When do we use this form of the spiccato?

A. We use it in slow quarter or eighth notes that are played forte or fortissimo or in a rather slow, "pesante" passage.

Practice this stroke using quarter notes, each note four times, in the form of scales or various finger patterns, gradually playing a bit faster using eighth notes.

Q. In what lane do we play the DRAMATIC SPICCATO bowing?

A. The general rule is that the spiccato bowings are played closer to the fingerboard than to the bridge, except in the higher positions. The higher the pitch, the closer the bow is drawn to the bridge.

Q. What do you call the second type of spiccato?

A. I have given it two names. One name is the LIGHT SPICCATO; the other name is the HAND AND FINGER SPICCATO.

Q. Why do you call it the hand and finger spiccato?

A. Simply because that is what we use to perform this type of spiccato. It requires an active motion of the hand and fingers and a passive action of the lower arm.

Q. In what part of the bow is this stroke played?

A. It is played between four and nine inches from the frog. This bowing is more difficult than the "dramatic" or "whole arm" spiccato. The exercise that I use for introducing the dramatic spiccato may also be used to teach the hand and finger spiccato.

Q. Does that mean that the small or PETITE MARTELÉ which uses about two inches of bow, forms the basis for the HAND AND FINGER SPICCATO?

A. Definitely. For elementary players, I would suggest playing eighth notes, each note four times, with a metronome marking of ♩ = MM 80.

For advanced players two- and three-octave scales would be a valuable way to practice. For very advanced players, even four-octave scales might be used.

Q. What lane would you use for the HAND AND FINGER SPICCATO?

A. Here it depends on the pitch. In the low positions, closer to the fingerboard. If you are to play softly, you might use the first lane. If you play loudly so that the stick is thrown from a greater height, it would be a bit closer to the bridge, or perhaps the second lane.

Q. When do you use the HAND AND FINGER SPICCATO?

A. When the music calls for spiccato bowing that is faster and lighter than the dramatic spiccato. The following example demonstrates the DRAMATIC SPICCATO and the HAND AND FINGER SPICCATO:

Beethoven, Symphony #5

It goes without saying that music for these bowings is usually marked with dots, and as a rule are eighth or sixteenth notes.

Q. How do we make a crescendo when we use the HAND AND FINGER SPICCATO?

A. That is a good question. The most important way is to make it slightly broader (a little less percussive). We can also throw the bow down on the string from a slightly greater height. What must be avoided is a scratchy tone. Be sure to pick the right lane for the best quality of tone.

Q. How much hair do we use?

A. For different volumes you might experiment with the amount of hair.

Q. What do you call the third type of spiccato?

A. Here again I have two names. The first name is the VERY LIGHT SPICCATO. The second name is the LOWER ARM SPICCATO. I prefer the LOWER ARM SPICCATO because the lower arm is the most active in this bowing.

Q. Should the hand and fingers be flexible for the lower arm spiccato?

A. Only slightly. You see, the bow is so flexible in the middle that we do not require much hand activity. The elbow, however, should be relaxed. The bow hold should be rather loose, and most of all, the elbow must open and close when we perform this bowing. We must experiment with the amount of hair to use in the lower arm spiccato.

Q. When do we use the LOWER ARM SPICCATO?

A. It is usually played in tempos ranging from ♩ = 84 to ♩ = 92. As a rule, it is used when we have sixteenth notes marked with dots. Most of the time, when the spiccato is played in a slower tempo, we are likely to do it closer to the frog, which would indicate the use of the hand and finger spiccato.

Q. What sensation should we experience when we use this lower arm spiccato in the middle of the bow?

A. The sensation of opening and closing the lower arm from the elbow joint. The upper arm should be as quiet as possible, used only when going from one string to another or when skipping strings. The elbow joint must feel as though it were well lubricated.

Q. How would you start teaching the VERY LIGHT or LOWER ARM SPICCATO?

A. In three stages. The first stage is as follows: play a series of eighth notes, with the middle of the bow striking the string. The bow should bounce straight up and down, with no lateral motion. This is accomplished by a rotary motion in the lower arm.

Q. In which lane should I strike the string?

A. In the second lane, near the fingerboard. Concentrate on exactly where you strike the string. Be sure that the bow strikes in the second lane all the time.

Q. Does that complete stage number one?

A. Yes. You are now ready for stage two which will produce the spiccato stroke.

Q. What should I concentrate on in stage two?

A. On the opening and closing of the right elbow, always striking the string in the same lane. Turn your head slightly and look at your elbow.

Q. My upper arm seems to be moving as I do this. How can I avoid this?

A. Lightly grip your upper arm with your left hand by bringing your left hand under the violin. If this is too difficult, here is a suggestion. Place your right elbow against a wall. This makes it easier to open and close the elbow while keeping the upper arm still.

Q. How fast should I do this?

A. In slow quarter notes, ♩ = MM 96. As soon as you are more confident of opening and closing the elbow, do it a bit faster. Do this on all strings, making sure that the right elbow is on a level with the top of the hand. After a week or two, the same exercise should be done all up-bows, and then all down-bows with a slight circular motion of the lower arm for each stroke. Do not permit the bow to strike below the middle or above the middle. Practice all up-bows and all down-bows until you are confident that you have freedom of motion in the lower arm from the elbow joint. Using all down-bows and then all up-bows with the slight circular motion is more in the nature of a preparatory study. When you alternate down-bows and up-bows, concentrate only on the slight opening and closing of the elbow.

Do not be discouraged with this bowing. It may take months to achieve. There is danger of striking two strings at the same time. It will be helpful to you to make sure that the bridge is properly curved at the top.

Q. What does the third stage consist of?

A. The third stage incorporates the use of the fingers of the left hand. That is, practicing scales in eighth notes, playing each note eight times, six times, four times, three times, and two times. As soon as you are more confident, play each note once.

As time goes on, you may be able to play scales in sixteenth notes at a tempo marking of ♩ = circa 84. After weeks or even months of practicing these three stages, we shall add a new dimension to the lower arm spiccato so that we may consider it an unusually fine lower arm spiccato. The ability to play the lower arm spiccato between one and two inches above the middle adds a new dimension.

Q. In what way?

A. It becomes lighter and you are able to do it a bit faster. But I remind you, you must be able to strike in the same lane for each bounce, and not allow it to go from one lane to another after every three or four bounces! This becomes a lifetime endeavor.

I also repeat that the main activity is in the lower arm from the elbow joint. I wish to add that this new dimension also includes playing from two to four inches below the middle for a heavier form of the lower arm spiccato.

Q. Why is it so important to be able to perform this stroke below the middle of the bow?

A. When you wish to play a bit louder or to reach a climax in a crescendo involving this lower arm spiccato, it is necessary to strike the string below the middle of the bow. However, below the middle of the bow it becomes increasingly difficult to confine the activity to the lower arm. It is important that the upper arm does not become active for this stroke, but there may be a slight sympathetic action of the upper arm.

It goes without saying that for the best quality of tone, the bow must strike the string parallel to the bridge, i.e. at right angles to the string.

Q. What do you call the fourth type of spiccato?

A. The FLYING SPICCATO. It consists of a series of spiccato notes in one bow, played up-bow most of the time.

Q. Can it also be played down-bow?

A. Yes, but it is a little more difficult. When the flying spiccato is played in a percussive manner, use as little bow as possible. Use a bit less hair for all of these flying spiccatos because they are played below the middle of the bow. If the music is marked forte use a bit more hair, the entire hand, lower arm, and upper arm in a well-coordinated manner.

If it is marked piano, use mostly the hand and the fingers, with a slight use of the upper arm. For dramatic passages in "fortissimo" play it close to the frog with practically all of the activity coming from the entire arm in the shoulder joint.

Flying spiccato

It is valuable to practice this stroke with the spiccato notes played in the same spot on the bow so that the bow recovers itself after each bow stroke.

Q. What do you call the fifth type of spiccato?

A. This type of spiccato is also called FLYING SPICCATO. The difference is in the way we start the series of spiccato notes. The first note of this group of flying spiccato notes is played smoothly with the bow already on the string.

Q. Why would we have to play that first note smoothly?

A. For various reasons. We may want to start the spiccato chain smoothly because it makes for a more graceful performance.

Another reason is that before you start the series of spiccato notes, you may be playing above the middle of the bow. To make it possible for you to carry the bow below the middle, you play the first note of the series smoothly, lifting the bow after it is played. When you arrive below the middle of the bow, it will then be easier to continue the series of spiccato notes off the string.

Q. What do you call the sixth type of spiccato?

A. I call it the EXPRESSIVE SPICCATO, but many teachers refer to it as the BRUSH SPICCATO.

Q. Is it also played below the middle?

A. Yes. In this form of spiccato you brush the string rather than strike it in a percussive manner. They may be played in single bows or a group in the same bow.

Q. Would that mean that you use more bow for each spiccato stroke?

A. Yes.

Q. When do you use this EXPRESSIVE SPICCATO?

A. When you play cantabile or espressivo passages, and you wish to lift the bow between the notes.

Q. How are these notes marked?

A. That brings up the problem of marking. Frequently, single eighth notes or quarter notes are marked with dots, but the emotional content of the work may call for the EXPRESSIVE SPICCATO. You could mark them with dashes, but most times dashes refer to a smooth détaché stroke. You will have to be content with possibly marking them with dots and dashes. It is up to the performer to determine which form is best.

I think that composers should write the word "spiccato" when they want the bow lifted from the string for each note.

Q. Would it be a good idea to present the various forms of the spiccato in outline form?

A. I agree. Here it is:
1. Dramatic Spiccato - played at or near the frog;
2. Hand and finger Spiccato - light spiccato, played 4 to 6 inches from the frog;
3. Lower Arm Spiccato - very light spiccato, played at the middle of the bow or one to two inches above the middle. Also to be played 2 to 4 jinches below the middle;
4. Flying Spiccato - played below the middle;
5. Flying Spiccato - the first note in the group played smoothly;
6. Expressive or Brush Spiccato - below the middle, with various bow lengths.

Q. What is your definition of the SAUTILLÉ?

A. It is a springing stroke derived from the SMALL DÉTACHÉ, played around the middle of the bow.

Q. Is this stroke frequently called the FAST SPICCATO?

A. Yes. I am not very content with this title because the basis for this stroke is a smooth détaché, whereas the basis for the spiccato is a small martelé. Another name given to this bowing is the natural spiccato.

Q. When do you introduce this bowing to a pupil?

A. From a technical standpoint, regardless of age, as soon as the pupil can play a smooth détaché in all parts of the bow. It derives from an active motion of the hand and fingers and a passive action of the lower arm. I would say that it would follow the spiccato.

Q. How would you start teaching this bowing?

A. Play a smooth détaché around the middle of the bow on a single note with only the hand and fingers. This may also be introduced on a double-stop on two open strings. There will be a passive action of the lower arm, but a concentration on the activity of the hand itself. Gradually allow the small détaché to be played faster and faster. If the hand is relaxed enough, the bow will rebound of its own momentum. Do this for only about four beats in sixteenth notes (♩ = MM 112). Then stop. Do a great many of these four-beat segments.

Q. Why only four beats?

A. Because if at the beginning you practice it for a longer period of time, you might allow your lower arm and hand to become tense. If you practice this regularly and do not become tense, the bow will gradually begin to rebound of its own momentum when you increase the speed.

Q. How much hair do I use for this stroke?

A. You must experiment with more or less hair. With some pupils the bow will bounce more readily using a bit more hair. There must be no upward pressure of the thumb.

Q. Can you describe the action of the hand itself in the performance of the SAUTILLÉ.

A. The hand moves in a manner that would form a combination of the vertical and the horizontal.

Q. If the bow does not spring of its own momentum, what are some of the suggestions you would offer?

A. One of the most important problems is the stiffening of the hand so that too much lower arm is used. There should be the right combination of vertical and horizontal hand action which will make it an oblique motion. Try practicing this small détaché about an inch below the middle. Try accenting the first of every four notes.

Q. Do we create this accent from the hand in the wrist joint?

A. No. The accent would not be strong enough. The impetus for this accent should come from the lower arm in the elbow joint.

Q. What sensation should I feel?

A. As though snapping a whip. The lower arm is the stick and the hand is the whip.

Q. A player may have both a heavy bow and a light bow. Can you offer any suggestion where on each bow the player should start practicing the sautillé?

A. One to three inches below the middle, and one to three or four inches above. There is really a more scientific way to locate the best spot. You must find the balancing point of each one of the bows.

Q. How do you find the balancing point?

A. Place the stick of the bow on the top of the first two fingers of the right hand until you find the fulcrum or spot where the bow will balance. Three or four inches above the balancing point in many instances will be the best spot to practice the sautillé.

Q. What about the balance of the right hand? Where should the weight of the hand be placed?

A. You may be able to get a fine bounce by allowing the center of balance or weight to be on the first finger. The lower part of the finger, between the base knuckle and the middle joint should be at right angles to the bow stick. Some pupils manage to get a better bounce by applying more weight of the hand to the little finger. For many players, it is advisable that the tip of the first finger relax its hold on the stick.

Q. Suppose I try these suggestions and I still cannot manage to have the bow leave the string?

A. In that case try slightly lowering the elbow so that the motion of the hand becomes more oblique. In other words, you are lowering the bow slightly toward the next higher string, and this changes the angle of the hand slightly.

Q. Is there another way to memorize the sensation of the combination of the vertical motion of the hand with the horizontal in order to get a successful sautillé bounce?

A. We might try this: play a series of sixteenth notes, four to a beat, where the first of each four is an open G string and the other three notes are on the open D string:

Try first playing this on the string with just a hand motion and only a passive use of the lower arm. Snap at the low G-string note. That snap can be done by whipping the lower arm with the hand into that motion and going directly to the D string. The transference from the G string to the D string must be done with the entire arm. Playing a series of these notes with a strong accent on the lower string can often create that rebounding from the string.

Q. When going from one string to another rapidly in this manner, do we use the full width of the hair?

A. That depends on the weight of the player's arm and the weight of the bow.

Q. Once we successfully develop this bounce, how do we go from one string to another?

A. In the sautillé bowing we go from one string to another by raising or dropping the entire arm so that the hand will be left free to continue the sautillé action.

Q. How high should the bow leave the string for the bounce?

A. That depends on the speed and the volume. Naturally, the higher the bounce, the slower the speed.

Q. In which lane should the sautillé bowing be played?

A. The general rule is that it should be played closer to the fingerboard than to the bridge. When the bounce is closer to the string it should be closer to the fingerboard. For the higher bounce you might try a higher lane. For the higher positions the bow is, of course, brought closer to the bridge. For velocity you should keep the bounce as close to the string as possible.

Q. What about the little finger during the sautillé bowing? Should it remain on the stick, or is it permitted to be removed?

A. That is an individual matter. I think you can get more control if the little finger remains on the stick. However, many fine performers remove the little finger and still achieve a fine sautillé. This deserves some experimentation.

Q. What is the next step in developing the sautillé bowing?

A. I would suggest a one-octave scale starting on open G, playing each note eight times. Accent the first of each four notes. Practice the same scale, as well as the following finger patterns each note four times, then two times. After a few weeks try playing each note three times, accenting the first of each group.

Our final goal is to be able to play the following patterns each note once, using the sautillé bowing. Of course the slurs and the quarter notes are to be eliminated.

Repeat each segment many times, gradually increasing the speed until the bow bounces of its own volition.

The above exercises are also extremely valuable for beginners to play in the following ways:

1. in quarter notes in separate bows (no slurs) above the middle and below the midde;
2. four to a bow in quarter notes;
3. four to a bow in eighth notes;
4. eight to a bow in eighth notes.

Q. Are there any other problems regarding the sautillé bowing?

A. Yes. Combining the various other bowings with the sautillé. Play the following exercise using the détaché on the eighth notes and the sautillé on the sixteenth notes:

Now, repeat this exercise but use the spiccato bowing on the eight notes and the sautillé bowing on the sixteenth notes:

Q. What type of spiccato should I use for the eighth notes?

A. Use the LOWER ARM SPICCATO (very light spiccato) for the eighth notes. These are played around the middle of the bow. It will not be too difficult then to go into the sautillé.

Q. Suppose the spiccato notes are to be played a bit louder?

A. In that case we use the HAND AND FINGER SPICCATO, which is played closer to the frog. This then presents the problem of moving the bow quickly toward the middle of the bow for the sautillé. These combinations require an unusually fine sautillé, which I shall talk about next.

Q. How would you define an UNUSUALLY FINE SAUTILLÉ?

A. When you can perform this bowing above the middle of the bow with a clearly articulated bounce that does not hop from one lane to another.

Q. How far above the middle should it be played?

A. As far above the middle as possible while still maintaining the bounce. Try first to bounce the bow an inch above the middle. Then two inches above the middle. That is not all. Now develop this sautillé an inch below the middle. For a more robust sautillé try for a bounce up to two, three, or four inches below the middle.

Q. Wouldn't that require a slight additional use of the lower arm?

A. Yes.

Q. How is the SAUTILLÉ GLISSANDO performed?

A. In the sautillé glissando the bow springs off the string exactly as it would in the regular sautillé. Here, the bow does the bouncing while the fingers of the left hand glide smoothly on the string with such speed that, for each bounce of the bow, each note sounds a half-step lower. In this type of sautillé, the left hand should be quite relaxed and should press the string only enough to articulate the notes. An interesting example of this is found in the Rondo Capriccioso of Saint-Saens. The joining of the glissando with the fingered chromatic scale must not be noticable.

The sautillé glissando, in general, should be practiced in groups of eight, six, four, three, and two, accenting the first note of each group.

Q. Is there a way to get more volume in a performance of the sautillé bowings?

A. Yes. Volume may be increased if you grip the bow a bit firmer and if you allow the bow to rebound from the string a bit higher. However, there is another way, and it then becomes another bowing with a different name.

Actually, it does not have to be called something else, but to be academically correct we will give it the name PICCHIETTATO. (It may also be spelled with only one "t.") The term PICCHIETTATO means "a bow that sounds as if it rebounds from the string". It is a general term. We will refer to this style of playing as a specific type of sautillé where the bow hair does not leave the string. Its character is that of a heavier type of sautillé, but without the bow coming off the string. Use the full width of the hair and grip the bow a bit more firmly. The picchiettato bowing allows us more dynamic variety in the use of the sautillé bowing.

Q. Is it also played above or below the middle as well as the middle?

A. Yes, but preferably a bit below the middle where we can get the benefit of a little more bow weight.

Q. Is the picchiettato more useful in orchestral playing?

A. Yes.

Q. Do you have any suggestions for coordinating the left-hand finger action with each bounce of the bow?

A. This is a life study. In performing the sautillé all of the left-hand finger tips should be closer to the strings. The third and fourth fingers should move quickly because they are more likely to be farther away from the strings.

Q. How would you define the SAUTILLÉ ARPEGGIO?

A. The SAUTILLÉ ARPEGGIO is a slurred bowing that is played over three or four strings. They are passages played so rapidly that the bow bounces of its own momentum.

An interesting example of the sautillé arpeggio may be found in the cadenza of the Violin Concerto in E minor by Mendelssohn.

Q. Do we start developing this bowing slowly as we did the sautillé?

A. Yes. The arpeggios are to be practiced slowly and as smoothly as possible. It is important that each note be equal in length and volume. The bow travels in a vertical curve and not in a straight line. You might want to call this the BARRIOLAGE or ROUND bowing. The bow must gradually move as closely as possible to the next string that is to be played. Each note will be even if the upper arm rises and falls the same distances with each bow stroke.

Q. When we play arpeggios, does the stick remain above the hair or does it tilt forward toward the fingerboard?

A. It is a bit more complicated than that. If you are playing a three-string arpeggio, starting down-bow you are permitted to tilt the stick a bit toward your face for the lowest note. On the middle note, the stick should be directly above the hair. On the highest note, the stick should be tilted slightly toward the fingerboard. For the four-string arpeggio the stick should be directly above the hair for the two middle strings.

Q. I realize that the string crossings are done with the upper arm. Are the right hand and fingers involved very actively?

A. That depends on the dynamic level. The greater the volume the firmer the bow hold becomes, and as a result the hand and fingers are less active.

The first finger, the thumb, and the little finger may pinch the stick a little bit to give it a rather firm hold. The real danger, however, is in the stiffening of the hand. The freedom of the hand should not be affected!

Q. How much bow do we use for the sautillé arpeggio?

A. We use about an inch or an inch and a half, around the middle of the bow. In the following exercises play each measure smoothly many times, starting slowly and gradually getting faster and faster. If the notes are evenly played, the bow will spring of its own momentum. If they are not played evenly, it might be impossible for the bow to rebound.

Q. In what lane do we practice this bowing?

A. In a lane that is closer to the fingerboard than to the bridge.

Q. Suppose the bow does not bounce? What do we do?

A. Try accenting the first of each six notes in the three-string arpeggios, and the first of each eight notes in the four-string arpeggios. The accent is created by a slight whipping motion of the lower arm. When you have achieved a springing bow in the three-string arpeggio, start practicing the four-string arpeggio.

Q. Don't we also accent the first note on the up-bow?

A. Yes. Many times this will help to get that bounce. Try accenting the first note of each bow change. A quick snapping of hand and forefinger may be very helpful.

Q. When we finally get a satisfactory spring, should we try to eliminate the accent on each group?

A. Yes. The accents should be considerably reduced depending on the musicality of the phrase. Sometimes a slight additional pressure of the first finger on the bow may help to regulate the bounce.

Q. Am I correct in assuming that for the string player, the term "staccato" has a specific meaning?

A. Yes. It means a series of martelé attacks in one bow, played to a great extent above the middle, up-bow and/or down-bow.

Q. What lane is the best for this staccato bowing?

A. As a general rule, a lane closer to the fingerboard than to the bridge. It goes without saying that from the fourth position and above, the bow is drawn more toward the bridge.

Q. How soon would you start this MARTELÉ STACCATO?

A. As soon as the pupil has a reasonably good martelé, which means a clean, precise martelé attack. This might be sometime during the second year. A suggested procedure would be as follows:

Place the tip of the bow on the G string, using the full width of the hair with the bow stick directly above. Pinch the bow with an upward pressure of the thumb so that the hair sets firmly into the string. Play a series of martelé attacks on the up-bow, using as little bow as possible for each attack. Do not go below the balancing point of the bow.

Q. How many martelé attacks should I attempt to get before I arrive at the balancing point?

A. About twenty. The object is to use as little bow as possible for each attack.

Q. What sensation should I experience?

A. A rotary motion of the lower arm from the elbow joint for each martelé attack. This makes it possible to transfer the weight of the arm to the first finger. The sensation to feel is a scooping motion of the hand or a pinch with no apparent length of the bow.

Q. Is it safe to say that all bow weight or pressure comes from the first finger?

A. No. The weight comes from a combination of the other fingers, the hand, and the lower arm, and is transferred to the first finger and then to the thumb acting as the counter force.

Q. Is it possible for every player to develop a VERY RAPID STACCATO?

A. Perhaps not.

Q. Should every player try to develop the VERY RAPID STACCATO?

A. Yes, if it is not overdone. I would suggest ten minutes at a time twice a day.

Q. How should I go about practicing this bowing?

A. Place the tip of the bow on the G string. Pinch the bow hair firmly into the string. Tense the entire arm from the top of the shoulder to the finger tips. Move the bow up-bow, but maintain the constant pressure on the string. Try to get as many compact rapid staccato notes in the smallest possible bow length.

Q. How would you describe the sensation?

A. That the entire arm is stiffened and made of one unit. The hand in the wrist joint does not necessarily have to be flexible. The rapid staccato cannot be created by a fast motion of the hand and wrist. The tension and the constant pressure create the sensation of quivering or trembling. It is really a nervous and spasmodic reaction to this constant pressure.

Q. Should I start practicing this slowly, gradually getting faster?

A. No. It should be practiced as rapidly as possible. Remember that there is very little relationship between the development of the martelé staccato and the rapid or nervous staccato.

Q. How do we practice the down-bow rapid staccato?

A. Very much the same way except that the stick is inclined toward the bridge.

Q. Do we turn the bow in the fingers?

A. No. We do not change the bow hold. The stick is inclined toward the player's face by lowering the wrist. The down-bow staccato is best performed in ascending passages.

Q. If I have a great deal of difficulty developing this bowing, can you offer any additional suggestions?

A. Experiment with more or less tension of the entire arm. Try tightening or lessening the pressure of each finger on the bow. The second and third fingers may frequently be removed to advantage so that you have a balance between the first and fourth fingers.

Try raising the right arm in the shoulder socket. Try changing the lane. Try drawing the bow so that it is not parallel to the bridge, which will mean that the right hand will be either farther from or closer to the body than usual.

Q. Is the down-bow staccato done only above the middle of the bow?

A. No. After some experience start practicing the down-bow staccato below the middle, gradually starting closer and closer to the frog.

Q. A number of teachers base the rapid staccato on the tremolo. Do you recommend this approach?

A. By all means. It is a very fine approach, and with many pupils it will work very well. I sometimes prefer it to other methods.

Q. How would you start teaching it?

A. Start in the middle of the bow, and play a small détaché as cleanly as possible. Gradually draw the bow closer and closer to the tip, maintaining a very rapid tremolo with the full width of the hair.

As you arrive at the tip, the tremolo should be played faster and faster. Then grip the bow a bit more firmly, tense the arm slightly, and begin to draw the bow slowly up-bow, using the lower arm making sure that the tremolo motion is maintained.

Q. What will happen?

A. Actually, what will happen is that you will hear every other note. That ends up in a sort of staccato that many players enjoy developing. Of course, it will not work with every student, but it is certainly worth trying.

Q. What is the FLYING STACCATO?

A. It is a series of staccato notes that are lifted from the string and played up-bow. Many teachers refer to it as the STACCATO VOLANTE.

Q. Where on the bow is this stroke played?

A. It depends on the speed of the passage. For a rapid and light flying staccato play in the upper third of the bow. For a fuller sound and a slower speed play in the middle third of the bow.

Q. How would you start teaching this bow stroke?

A. Place the bow about two or three inches from the tip with the full width of the hair on the string. Practice passages similar to the following:

Play the first note with the bow hair set well into the string, but permit the bow to come off the string for the remaining succession of notes.

Q. How do we accomplish that?

A. Each note is created by an energetic force which may come from the hand and arm, but the first note is started with an especially firm impetus. Do not lessen the hold on the bow throughout the series of notes.

Q. Have you any suggestions if one has difficulty with this stroke?

A. Try placing the first finger on the bow about an inch away from the second finger. Make sure that the fingers maintain a firm hold on the bow stick. Experiment with more or less tension in the hand and forearm. As in the rapid staccato, try changing the lane or drawing the bow at different angles from the bridge.

Q. Do we perform this bowing below the middle of the bow?

A. Yes. When you play this stroke below the middle, it is usually slower, louder, and more intense.

Q. What is the difference then between the FLYING STACCATO and the FLYING SPICCATO?

A. The FLYING SPICCATO is played quite a bit slower and softer, with a relaxed arm and a good coordination and flexibility between the upper and lower arm and the hand. With the FLYING STACCATO the entire arm is more tense and moving as one unit.

Q. If a pupil does not successfully perform this stroke, do you have an alternative approach?

A. Yes. The alternative is worthwhile experimenting with. What may work with one player may not work with another.

First play the flying staccato stroke at the middle, all up-bows, in eighth notes. Then do it starting two inches above the middle, and then three or four inches from the tip, and then at the tip, with all up-bows.

Q. Do you strike the string with the flat of the hair?

A. Yes. Perhaps a little less than the full width of the hair, but I would think most of the time it can be done with the full width of the hair.

Q. Do we strike the string at a 90-degree angle?

A. Not always, experiment with the various angles.

Q. Do we hold the stick as firmly as possible?

A. Yes. However, you must experiment with the degree of firmness. Some players will be more successful if they pinch the bow a little more firmly, with the third and fourth fingers and a little lighter with the first and second fingers.

Q. What can we do to achieve greater velocity with this stroke?

A. When you wish to increase the velocity, move the forearm slowly and in not too relaxed a manner. Third and fourth fingers then will apply a firmer pressure on the bow stick. This will help the spring of the bow.

Q. When I want to move really fast, what will I do?

A. The bouncing must become more compact. Naturally, you have to reduce the height of the bow on the string. Do not relax the arm between strokes as you would in performing the FLYING SPICCATO. There should be slightly more tension in the lower arm. I would describe it as mild tension.

The faster you play, the closer the bow hair should be to the string. Lift the bow from the string as little as possible. The idea is that the bow has to continue to hop along the string in the manner a stone would skip across water if you throw a flat stone across a lake. Play as many notes as possible in one bow. You can start near the tip and go to a little below the middle.

Q. When I start a passage of the flying staccato that is rapid, do I bounce the first note or should I start on the string?

A. One should be able to do it both ways. You should start such a passage with the bow on the string and lift that note to give the impetus to bounce the others in a very compact manner.

You can start it by actually striking the very first note from a small height. The important thing is to experiment with just how much finger pressure to apply on the bow and how much tension is to be applied with arm.

Q. What is the difference between the RICOCHÉT and the FLYING STACCATO?

A. First the similarities:
1. They are both played around the middle of the bow, a bit below for more volume and a bit above for more delicate passages.
2. They both come off the string and are played quite rapidly.
3. Both include a series of notes played in one bow.

The main differences between the two bowings are as follows:
1. For the ricochét, the bow is held rather firmly and thrown on the string.
2. At the instant the bow strikes the string the strength of the bow hold is considerably lessened and the bow is permitted to rebound by its own volition.

For the FLYING STACCATO, it is best if the bow is on the string for the first note and comes off for the remaining succession of notes. The bow hold is not lessened during the performance of the flying staccato.

With many bows the ricochét will be more readily acquired if the stick, itself, is turned just a bit so that more of the hair strikes the string.

Once the bow strikes the string for the ricochét, the grip is relaxed and the bow bounces of its own energy. The bounce is not created by impulses imparted to the bow by the hand. Most of the time with the ricochét, or as it is sometimes called, the THROWN STACCATO, all the notes are played because of the bounce that is created by the initial throw. We refer to this as the "short ricochét." The reason that we call it the "short ricochét" is that all the notes can be played without any additional energy.

Q. Suppose we have many notes in the bow that are to be "ricochéted," so to speak?

A. We refer to this as the "long ricochét," which includes a great number of notes in one stroke. We naturally start out by striking the string in the same manner as though we were to play only a few notes. During the long ricochét a diminuendo takes place while we still have some notes to play. If the diminuendo is such that we do not hear the notes loudly enough, we consciously and deliberately include some additional action of the arm to keep the bow springing during the remainder of the stroke.

Q. How would you teach the RICOCHÉT?

A. Hold the bow firmly with the hair of the bow about one inch above the string. Throw the bow down on the string, releasing most of the hold on the bow as soon as the bow strikes the string. Allow the bow to bounce by itself, using as little bow length as possible from the elbow joint. To develop a more colorful ricochét, experiment by dropping the bow on the string from different heights.

It is possible to begin the stroke by playing one-octave scales in the first position in the following rhythms:

Use no more than one inch of bow for the down-bow and practically no bow at all for the up-bow. Pinch the bow slightly to stop the rebounds. The bounce is faster near the point, and becomes gradually slower and louder as you play nearer the middle of the bow. Experiment with the various lanes for quality and volume.

Q. What is the difference between the TREMOLO and the SAUTILLÉ?

A. The SAUTILLÉ comes off the string while the TREMOLO remains on the string.

Q. Would you say then that the basis for the tremolo is the small détaché?

A. Yes. A small détaché played as rapidly as possible using the hand and fingers with some action of the lower arm.

Q. What part of the bow is used for the tremolo?

A. If the passage is marked "forte", the tremolo is played around the middle or above the middle of the bow. For softer passages play closer to the tip. In "piano" passages use as little bow as possible with each note clearly articulated. Most tremolo passages should start with a slight accent even if it is not marked.

Q. Even in passages marked "piano"?

A. Yes. However, if the passages are marked "forte," use more bow for the initial note. This will mean some use of the lower arm. Many players improve their tremolo by removing the little finger from the bow.

Q. What is the SUL PONTICELLO stroke?

A. It is a stroke played as close as possible to the bridge. It may be helpful to hold the bow a bit looser than usual.

Q. What sensation should I feel when I play sul ponticello?

A. The sensation of using the full width of the hair with a few of the hairs actually on the bridge.

Q. What is it supposed to sound like?

A. Very whistly, a bit nasal and glassy. An eerie sound that may send some shivers up your spine. You will hear a good many of the upper partials.

Q. Sometimes I fail to hear the fundamental notes. Is it always necessary to tell whether the note is in tune?

A. Not always, but the chances are that it will be in tune. When composers combine the tremolo and the sul ponticello bow strokes, they are more interested in hearing the upper partials. If the notes are not tremolo but longer in length, the fundamental notes are more important. You will then move a bit away from the bridge with some slight additional bow pressure. You must not, however, lose the ponticello effect.

Q. What comments can you offer on the SUL TASTIERA bowing?

A. This bowing is played very near (with some passages on) the fingerboard. Here again the bow must be held a bit looser than usual.

Q. How do we perform the COL LEGNO bowing?

A. We create the sound by tapping the string with the bow stick.

Q. What part of the bow stick strikes the string?

A. Anywhere from a bit below the middle to near the tip of the bow, depending upon the volume desired and the speed of the notes.

Q. How do we hold the bow for this stroke?

A. We tilt the bow stick by lowering the wrist joint. This permits the stick to face the bridge. The tapping is done by a slight rotary motion of the lower arm in the elbow joint with the hand participating in a very active manner.

Q. In what lane do we strike the string?

A. That depends on the type of sound that we desire. There is a vast difference between the sound produced near the fingerboard and that produced near the bridge.

It is often used in a ricochét type of passage:

Q. What is the PAGANINI bowing?

A. In this stroke we have a single note in one bow followed by two notes in one bow. The single note is always played down-bow and occurs on a different beat each time:

Q. What is the VIOTTI bow stroke?

A. The VIOTTI bowing includes two MARTELÉ notes in a single-bow stroke. The bow change is always on a weak beat or the off-beat. It has a charm of its own if the second note in the bow is accented.

How to Produce a Beautiful Tone

Q. When do you start discussing beautiful tone production with the students?

A. Before the pupils draw the very first bow stroke you should play a series of long notes of different qualities. They should range from scratchy sounds to beautiful tones.

Discuss the different types of sounds, and impresss upon the pupils the importance of memorizing the sensation of a beautiful tone.

I would say to older or more advanced students, "You must first hear in your mind the type of sound that you want to produce on the instrument. In other words, you must choose the type of sound that will satisfy your expressive need."

If you listen to various artists, you will become aware of the differences in their sounds. Each performer will produce a very beautiful sound that is distinctive. You must decide which sound you would consider ideal and would like to emulate. You can accomplish this by attending live performances and listening to recordings.

Q. When players have a mental concept of a beautiful sound, how do they produce it?

A. Producing the sound is a sensation. That sensation is one of pulling or drawing the tone from the instrument rather than pressing it out. That is a knack that players must discover through practice and experimentation.

Here is an exercise that will be helpful in memorizing that sensation, and also help to develop a well-controlled bow arm:

Draw the bow ½ inch above the string for eight slow beats. In your attempt to maintain the height of just ½ inch above the string throughout the stroke, you are memorizing the sensation of drawing a beautiful sound. Drawing, and not pressing, the tone out encourages the instrument to speak for itself.

Q. Have you other exercises that will help to memorize the sensation of drawing a beautiful sound?

A. You can memorize that sensation by playing artificial harmonics holding each note from four to eight beats.

Q. Do you have any suggestions for developing a beautiful tone in the high positions?

A. In the high positions there must be less bow weight on the string. The higher the pitch, the lighter the bow pressure should be. But while doing this, the fingers of the left hand must apply firmer pressure on the string. I might summarize by saying that in the high positions we play double piano with the bow, and double forte with the left hand.

Q. What are the factors that go into the production of a beautiful sound?

A. If we analyze a sound, we find that there are four important elements to consider:
1. bow speed;
2. bow pressure or weight;
3. lane — by lane I mean that point on the string where the bow is drawn;
4. pitch, or the length of the string.

Q. What do you mean by the length of the string?

A. If we play a note higher in pitch, the string becomes shorter. By length I mean the distance between the finger on the string and the bridge.

Q. What do you mean by the term "lane"?

A. Let us divide the length of the string between the end of the fingerboard and the bridge into five equal points of contact. We will refer to each point of contact as a "lane."

Lane #1 is at the fingerboard, but not on it.

Lane #2 is near the fingerboard, midway between the center and the fingerboard.

Lane #3 is midway between the fingerboard and the bridge. (the center lane)

Photo No. 34A

Lane #4 is near the bridge, midway between the center and the bridge.

Lane #5 is at the bridge, but not on it.

Photo No. 34B   **Photo No. 34C**

Q. What are the general rules that will guide us in the choice of lanes?

A. Here are some of the general principles that will determine the lane to be used.

If you remain in the same lane and wish to play louder, you must increase the speed of the bow. If you wish to remain in the same lane and play softer, you must apply less pressure and move the bow slower.

Let us suppose you wish to maintain the same speed of the bow and to play louder. You will then have to increase the pressure. However, as you increase the pressure or bow weight, you will have to move to a higher lane which will be closer to the bridge.

If you wish to maintain the same speed of the bow and want to play softer, you will have to decrease the pressure on the bow. In order to do that, you must leave that lane and move to a new lane closer to the fingerboard.

If you want to maintain the same volume and move the bow faster (as in fast quarter notes) you will leave that lane and move the bow closer to the fingerboard.

If you want to maintain the same volume or the same bow pressure and want to move the bow slower, you will have to move the bow close to the bridge.

Q. Is it possible to achieve the best possible sound in more than one lane?

A. Not really. There is only one lane where you can produce the best tone quality. It is up to you to find that lane. Frequently, you will produce a reasonably good tone quality. However, you must not be content with that. You should always experiment with another lane. By experimenting with another lane or lanes, you will be able to produce the best tone quality. It is up to you to find that lane. Frequently, you will produce a reasonably good tone quality.

The general rule is that for every type of sound, every style of bowing, there is only one lane that produces the best quality of sound.

Q. What is the relationship between the lanes and the various styles of bowings?

A. Here it is in outline form. You will play in the center lane or closer to the fingerboard when you play:
1. long notes that are soft;
2. short notes that are soft (hand and finger stroke);
3. short notes that are loud;
4. martelé strokes;
5. spiccato strokes;
6. sautillé strokes;
7. ricochét strokes;
8. three- or four-voice chords that are short and played simultaneously;
9. notes that are marked sforzando.

Q. If I wish to produce more volume with the spiccato, sautillé or ricochét bowings, I would naturally bounce the bow from a greater height above the string. Would I then go to a higher lane closer to the bridge?

A. Yes. By all means.

120

Q. As a general rule, when shall I play closer to the bridge?

A. You will draw the bow closer to the bridge when you play:
1. long notes that are loud;
2. three- or four-voice chords that are sustained. The two lower notes will be played near the fingerboard, while the two upper notes will be sustained near the bridge.

Q. What is the relationship between the pitch and the lane?

A. All the bowings that I have listed as being played in the middle or near the fingerboard are played gradually closer to the bridge when the pitch is higher.

Q. Do you mean in terms of higher positions?

A. Yes. A passage in the first position may be played beautifully near the fingerboard, but the same passage on a lower string in the fifth position will have to be played nearer to the bridge. It is interesting to note that on all the string instruments, even in the first position, the bow will have to be drawn a bit closer to the bridge when playing on the highest string. The higher the pitch, the closer the bow is drawn to the bridge.

Q. When you talk about the fast-bow stroke, how does the player avoid that whistley or "surfacy" sound that sometimes results?

A. The fast-bow stroke is probably one of the most important strokes on any string instrument. To improve the quality of the fast-bow stroke you must do two things:
1. avoid leaving the lane that produces the best sound — this may mean a lane that is a bit closer to the fingerboard;
2. apply a bit more finger pressure on the bow (also called pinching the bow) to avoid the whistley effect that is frequently heard when the bow is drawn very rapidly.

Q. What does pinching the bow accomplish?

A. It gives the player more control.

Q. Does it also mean more pressure of the hair on the string?

A. No, because on the fast bow stroke you will frequently lighten the bow pressure on the string. If you play a dotted half note followed by a quarter note in 4/4 time, you will notice that you get the best quality of tone if the dotted half note is played closer to the bridge and the fast-bow quarter note is played closer to the fingerboard.

Just how close you will draw the bow to the bridge and then to the fingerboard depends on the dynamic level. Play one-octave scales with one long note and then one short note, using the entire bow for each note.

Here is an example of this type of bowing:

W. B. 1st position - complete the scale

near the bridge - near the fingerboard

Complete the scale remaining in the same position

Q. Should scales like these be practiced in various positions?

A. Yes. Make sure that the bow is always parallel to the bridge on the fast bow strokes, and that there is no "surfacy" or whistley sound. The whistley sound may be an indication that you are in the wrong lane.

Q. Would you say that a performer should always plan the proper lane even before starting to play?

A. Yes. Much thought should also be given as to just how to start the bow stroke.

Q. What are the different ways to start a bow stroke?

A. There are three ways to start a bow stroke, and you must become proficient in each one of them. The first way is to start with the bow on the string before the tone begins.

The second way is as follows: the bow is placed on the string, then pressed into the string in preparation for a martelé attack. This may vary from very light to heavy.

The third way is to drop the bow on the string from above in a circular motion.

Q. Do you mean that the bow is actually in motion before it touches the string?

A. That is correct, but in a circular manner. At the bottom of the curve the bow contacts the string and keeps moving.

Q. When we drop the bow on the string, how is that done? With the entire arm or with the fingers?

A. Either way is correct. If you wish to use only the fingers, hold the bow about ¼ inch above the string. Using only the fingers, drop the bow gently on the string. As soon as the bow touches the string, start drawing the bow.

When you start a bow stroke with the martelé accent you will approach the string with the entire arm.

Q. How can I acquire a big tone?

A. Play long notes loudly, holding each note for six beats. Apply an accent on the beginning of each beat with the tone sounding thoughout. The bow must remain firmly in motion without any interruption in the sound. I call this bowing the STRONG LEGATO ACCENT.

Q. How can I produce these accents?

A. By moving the bow more rapidly and applying more weight to the bow at the start of each beat.

Q. By more weight do you mean weight of the arm, or more pressure of the thumb and first finger?

A. Whatever pressure is exerted on the string is transferred through the first finger. If the tone is forced, it is probably due to the bow not being drawn quickly enough. If you have a concept of a beautiful sound, you will be less likely to force the tone.

Q. At what tempo would you suggest producing these six accents?

A. ♩ = 50. These should be done for a number of weeks.

Q. What should I play?

A. First, start on open strings, then one-octave scales. Then two-octave scales, and eventually three-octave scales. For more advanced players there is a great advantage in playing three-octave scales because the different points of contact (or lanes) must be considered. The higher the pitch, the closer the bow must be drawn to the bridge.

Q. How will this help me to develop a big tone?

A. At this point I will ask you to play these notes for six beats each loudly enough to maintain the sound of the accent at its loudest point, without lowering the volume between each beat.

I might say that it is the leveling or equalizing of the volume at the height of the accent. You must memorize not only the way the hand feels when it produces the six accents, but you must memorize the sound at the loudest level, and then sustain that sound. You will then be drawing a big sound.

Q. What other exercises have you to develop a big sound?

A. Play a scale fortissimo, holding each note for eight beats, while you:
1. apply as much pressure as possible,
2. move the bow as slowly as possible,
3. play as close to the bridge as possible.

Q. Suppose the sound is scratchy or forced. What should I do?

A. You may have to move the bow faster. Try not to apply less bow pressure. The tone quality must not be impaired.

Another good exercise is as follows:

Place the frog of the bow on the lowest string, pinching the bow hair into the string. Draw the bow quickly and firmly to 6 inches from the tip, but do not release the bow pressure on the string. Rather, add more weight after you pass the middle. Lift the bow and return to the frog as quickly as possible, making a complete circle with the arm. Pinch the bow hair into the string again and repeat, playing a scale in half notes in this manner. Start each note in the second lane (near the fingerboard) and sustain each note in the fourth lane (near the bridge.)

Q. Are there any special bow studies to aid in the maintaining of a big sound while changing strings?

A. Yes. Place the frog of the bow on the E string (or highest string) with the right thumb bent outward, and the little finger well curved. The right elbow should be about 3 or 4 inches from the body, forming a straight line with the top of the hand.

Using only the fingers, raise the bow until the hair touches the A string. Go back to the E string by lowering the fingers. Do this six times without moving the elbow or arm. Practice this on all strings.

Q. Are there any other exercises for developing a big sound?

A. Here is an excellent one:

Start in the first lane. Draw the whole bow slowly for eight beats in the first lane, applying enough bow pressure to completely crush the tone. Do this for a few bow strokes.

Gradually draw the whole bow faster and faster until you achieve the finest tone quality. You will discover the maximum amount of pressure and bow speed you must apply in order to get the finest quality of sound while playing as loudly as possible. Do the same thing in each of the five lanes.

Q. Is there a visual method by which we can develop a large, even sound?

A. Yes. Place the frog of the bow on the lowest open string. Start with a martelé accent and draw the bow fortissimo for eight beats, using the whole bow.

While doing this, look carefully at the vibrating string. The amplitude of the vibration is at its widest when you play fortissimo. This is very easily seen.

If, as you watch it, the amplitude is the same from the frog to the tip, it proves to you that the tone is even and large.

If the amplitude narrows on the way to the tip, you know that the tone is not even. The only way to correct it is to apply more bow weight.

Q. Shall I apply this visual exercise to all the lanes?

A. Yes.

Q. Exactly how do we apply the different bow weights to the strings?

A. At the frog, or below the middle, the weight is applied by the entire arm, more or less, depending upon the volume.

As we approach the middle on the down-bow, the weight comes from the lower arm, with a gradual inward turning of the lower arm at the elbow joint, i.e. a rotary motion of the lower arm in the elbow joint.

The weight is then gradually transmitted to the first finger which, of course, supplies that weight from the different parts of the arm. At the very tip of the bow, however, the weight would actually have to be supplied from the hand itself.

Q. Is the degree of firmness with which we hold the bow to be altered to any extent when we play very loudly?

A. It is a mistake when we wish to play with a big sound to grip the bow more firmly or to tighten the fingers on the bow. This creates tension, and it can be a great disadvantage.

Learning How to Sight Read

Q. How soon should we train students to sight read?

A. Actually, after a few months of study, students should be told about the importance of sight reading. They should be given specific exercises to help them become good sight readers.

Q. What is the most important sensation to memorize in order to become a good sight reader?

A. The ability to read ahead.

Q. Aren't many students hesitant to read ahead for fear of losing their place?

A. With some training, students can widen their peripheral vision so that they can read ahead and not lose their place.

Q. How does sight reading benefit our playing in general?

A. It gives players more confidence and enjoyment. In a subtle way it makes it possible for a player to develop greater velocity.

If we take two players, equally talented, musically and technically, one may develop more velocity than the other purely because of wider peripheral vision.

Q. At the elementary level, how do we go about teaching students to memorize the sensation of looking ahead?

A. I will say to the pupil, "Let us pick a melody. Play the first two measures. When you arrive at the third measure, turn away quickly from the music and look upward. Play the first note in the third measure. You are now memorizing the sensation of reading ahead."

Every pupil will be able to do that without difficulty. It is important that their first attempt at sight reading be a successful experience.

"Play the first and second measures again. Now turn away at the third measure and play the first two notes of the third measure. Then three notes, and eventually the entire measure. In this way you are developing the skill of looking ahead and widening your peripheral vision."

You must motivate your students to train themselves in this manner a few times each week. They will get to the point where they will enjoy practicing sight reading.

"Put an "X" over the fourth measure. Play the first and second measures again. Look away, and attempt to play the first note of the fourth measure. Do the same with other measures on the line. Try playing the last measure on the line and possibly the first and second notes on the next line. With a little practice it is amazing how your sight reading ability will increase."

Know that it is possible to motivate pupils to enjoy this type of experience. This can be done with familiar and unfamiliar melodies. It will be more valuable to play melodies that are less familiar.

Q. How can I motivate players in an orchestra to watch the conductor?

A. While the orchestra plays, the conductor will do the following: change the tempo, suddenly or gradually, and insist that the orchestra follow very carefully. Suddenly stop! If the students are watching, they will stop with the conductor. With some practice, performers in an orchestra should be able to read their music and watch the conductor by widening their peripheral vision.

Q. Do you have any physical exercises that will help to widen one's peripheral vision?

A. Yes. Here are three exercises:
1. Place the first finger of each hand on the high cheek bone on each side of your face. Now move the fingers in front of you to about eight inches in front of our face, maintaining the same distance between each finger. Without moving your head, look from one finger to the other. Do this in slow half notes, several times a day, ♩= Circa MM 96.

Photo No. 35

Now separate the fingers to a distance of 12 inches. Look from one finger to the other four times, without moving the head.

Next, separate the fingers to 14 inches apart, and repeat the exercises without moving the head. Gradually continue to increase the distance between the fingers until you reach a distance of about 26 inches. You are now widening your peripheral vision. Do this in quarter in this tempo, ♩ = circa MM 69.

Photo No. 36

2. Place the first finger of the right hand between your eyes, four inches in front of your nose. The finger tip should point toward the ceiling. Place the first finger of the left hand at arm's length in a straight line in front of the right hand. Now look directly at the first finger of the right hand (which is four inches in front of your nose). While you are doing this, can you see two fingers on the left hand? If you succeed in seeing two fingers on the left hand (and you must concentrate on

Photo No. 37

the finger of the right hand exclusively) the right finger will seem to be in the center of what appears to be the two fingers of the left hand. Hold this for eight slow counts, ♩ = circa MM 84. If you are successful in this eye calisthenic, you are strengthening the eye muscles and widening your peripheral vision.

3. Roll your eyes in complete circles, clockwise for eight slow counts, ♩ = circa MM 50. Repeat this exercise counter clockwise. Do not move your head.

Photo No. 38

Q. What suggestions will you offer to a performer (at any level) who is about to go for an audition?

A. Since sight reading plays an important part in most auditions, consider carefully the following suggestions.

1. When a piece of music is placed in front of you to sight read, you are allowed a few moments to look it over. Use this time before you begin to play.
2. Look at the key signature and the tempo markings.
3. Locate the fast passages. Try to set your tempo according to the difficulty of any of the fast passages. This is not always permitted, but it is worth trying.
4. If a passage is to be played an octave higher than written and you are a bit hesitant to try it, play it "loco."
5. If there are changes in tempo throughout the page, make sure that you know where these changes occur. Observe them as you scan the page.
6. It takes a few moments to observe the dynamic marks. Look them over so that you become familiar with them. Look for long crescendi. Look for sudden "fortes" or "pianos." In a very few moments you can get a rather good idea of the dynamic marks of idea of the dynamic marks of the music as well as its structure.
7. Locate all the repeat marks and observe them.
8. Once you start playing you are never to stop or slow down.
9. No matter how difficult a passage is, do not alter or repeat it.

10. It is wise, when you sight read, to leave out various embellishments, such as grace notes, mordants, turns, or short trills if they trouble you. Of course, if you can play them without slowing the tempo, do so. However, you must get in the spirit of the music.

11. Do not insist on playing all the notes in difficult passages. If you play the first two beats of a measure, and find that the next one or two beats consist of the very difficult run, it would be better to leave it out in order to make sure that you come in on time in the next measure.

12. At home sight read a new piece with a metronome set at a convenient tempo. Force yourself to stick to the tempo.

Q. Should amateur players try to become good sight readers?

A. By all means. When they are good sight readers, they can enjoy playing chamber music as well as playing in community orchestras. It adds a great deal to their lives. Good sight readers are very likely to continue playing their instruments after their student years.

If you teach young people to sight read, you are giving them a heritage that will last for the rest of their lives. As people live longer, their happiness is dependent on their resources. Making music together can be one of the most inspiring and enjoyable activities at any age.

Some Basic Principles of Musicianship
The Art of Interpreting Music

Q. Is it necessary for players to study the principles of interpretation?

A. Yes, by all means!

Q. But aren't talented players instinctively aware of these principles?

A. To a great extent there is a science to the art of interpretation, the knowledge of which will confirm the performer's instincts.

Q. Will it help performers who are not very gifted?

A. The performer without a great technical aptitude can become sensitively aware of the interpretive stimuli.

Q. If a player follows all the marks the composer has placed in the music, wouldn't that be considered a musical performance?

A. To a great extent it would. However, a really fine interpreter is one who includes in the performance many nuances that have not been written on the page by the composer. It is that which is not written in the music that makes for a great performance. We may use the terms "unwritten crescendo," "unwritten diminuendo," etc.

Q. What are the fundamental principles which will enhance the performance of a piece of music?

A. I will express some of these principles by starting with the very basics.

We all know that the scale (or tonality) has seven notes, with each note possessing a dynamic force. This force includes tones that are rest tones and those that are active enough to lead or progress to the rest tones.

Another very important element in interpretation is the accent, i.e. the force that is applied to any note or beat.

Q. How many types of accents do you refer to?

A. There are three type of accents:
1. the metric accent, which occurs at the beginning of each measure so that the listener is aware of the bar;
2. the rhythmic accent, which has to do with the phrase; when this is applied skillfully, the listener is permitted to feel or become cognizant of the beginning and end of each phrase — this may occur in any part of a measure;
3. the expressive accent — this accent is placed on a note that has poetic or emotional significance.

Q. Am I correct in saying that the expressive accent may not be used at regular intervals?

A. Yes. The performer is guided by the emotional content of the work.

Q. Why don't composers mark the various accents?

A. In my opinion it would be asking too much from the composer to mark these three different types of accents throughout the music. You know that the metrical accent is very obvious. The performers should know by studying the music where to place the rhythmical accents. When it comes to the placing of the expressive accents, the performers must be guided by their own musical taste, which can be cultivated to a great extent.

Q. Can we have expressive accents on a number of notes in succession?

A. Yes. They may be applied on several notes that follow each other. An expressive accent may be placed on any beat, whether primary or secondary. Expressive accents may be placed in any part of a phrase — even on the last note. They may fall on repeated notes, or notes that are unusually discordant.

Q. Is is possible then for a certain note to receive an accent for more than one reason?

A. Yes. It can receive a metrical accent for being the first note of the measure. At the same time, we might want to apply additional emphasis because the note is emotionally significant or because it is a reiterated note.

Q. Can you give an example of this?

A. In the following example emphasis is applied to the first note of the second measure because it is a reiterated note:

Ex. No. 1

Q. Is there a general rule that applies to reiterated notes?

A. If a note is repeated, the first note falling on a weak beat and the second note falling on a strong beat, we apply additional emphasis on the strong beat because it is a reiterated note.

Another example (Ex. No. 2) is from the Concerto in A Minor by Vivaldi:

When we have a long note in a measure, it should be accented, particularly if it falls on the first beat. The longer the note is held, the more emphasis we place on it:

A series of notes, each of which is followed by a short rest, should be accented, whether they are on or off the beat:

Q. Can you cite an example of a note that is accented because it begins a phrase?

A. In the following example I accent the first note of each phrase, even though it falls on a weak beat:

Q. Can you provide another example where an accent is placed on a weak beat?

A. If a beat is divided into several notes, you should consider accenting the first note of that divided beat, even if it falls on a weak beat:

If the last note of a measure is a quarter note, and if that note is preceded by eighth or sixteenth notes, you will accent the quarter note even though it is a weak beat.

132

Q. Do we apply accents to notes that are held over to the next measure?

A. Yes. In the following example we have a note that is strongly accented because that note is held over through the first beat of the next measure:

Q. Would you apply an accent on a note that is held over through the next beat regardless of what part of the measure it occurs?

A. Yes. We will also place an accent on a note that is prolonged throughout the next beat. This may occur in any part of the measure.

Bach, Concerto in A Minor

Q. Why is phrasing such a problem for string players?

A. When string music is edited, slurs are frequently indicated for bowing or technical convenience. Often, to achieve that convenience, the beginnings and endings of phrases are overlooked. In performance the listener must be cognizant of the first and last note of each phrase. This must be made clear, as punctuation marks clearly designate each sentence in prose. The first note and the last note of a phrase may be found on an accented beat or on an unaccented beat. The first note of a phrase may be found on any fraction of a beat, but the last note of a phrase is usually found on the beginning of a beat.

In the following example the beginning of the phrase falls on the second half of the first beat, but the ending falls on the beginning of a beat:

Moderato

Q. How would you describe the different types of phrases?

A. I would compare musical phrases to different types of sentences in prose. In a musical phrase comparable to a declarative sentence in prose, we would play the last note a bit softer, just as we would lower the voice on the last word. In many instances the last note is somewhat shortened in order to leave a slight pause or breath before starting the next phrase.

On the other hand, there are certain sentences where we should raise the voice as we would in interrogatory or exclamatory sentences.

It is interesting to notice that the vocalist is guided by the words of a piece of music. String players do not have that guidance. The following will represent endings where the last note should be softer than the preceeding note:

Q. Is there a general rule regarding the application of expressive accents?

A. They do not fall at regular intervals. We now enter into a world where we speak of poetic expression. Here, there are no set rules. These accents supply poetic coloring and must be felt by the performer.

Q. Is there a great difference of opinion as to when these expressive accents are to be applied?

A. Definitely. There is no regularity as to where to place them, but what I refer to as "The Magnetized Note" offers some guidance.

Q. What do you mean by "the magnetized note"?

A. In every phrase there is usually one note that should be given more prominence. We must play in such a manner that the listener feels drawn to that note, which I like to call "the magnetized note."

Q. How can that be done?

A. This may be achieved by a slight crescendo, slight accelerando, or ritard. By our performance the listener must definitely be aware that we have reached the "magnetized note."

Q. What are the possible ways to perform the magnetized note?

A. When you reach the magnetized note, you might vibrate on it more intensely, play it a bit louder, or slightly prolong that note.

Q. Are subtle changes in tempo always involved in approaching the magnetized note?

A. Very frequently, but not always.

Q. When we have a series of expressive accents, would we then introduce these subtle tempo changes?

A. By all means. In the following example we have a series of expressive accents. You might want to play them with greater animation and energy. You might play either a bit faster or a bit slower. You might introduce rubato. In the following example, you may feel the desire to make a slight accelerando:

accel.

Q. In general, can you offer any guidelines as to when to make ritards?

A. Ritards are desirable under the following conditions:
1. when we play a lengthy passage that is quick or lively and includes a long diminuendo;
2. on a series of long notes that are strongly accented;
3. when we return to the main theme or as we approach a recapitulation section;
4. frequently in a transition to a different time;
5. where we have a well-marked crescendo which is used to introduce an important passage;
6. in a passage leading to an espressivo section:
7. at the end of a long trill;
8. when we approach a fermata;
9. when we have a series of ornamental notes that embellish a melody; it would sound too hurried if we played these notes in strict time; a slight ritard on these ornamental notes would be in order, and this could come under the heading of poetic license;
10. when the performer plays in an ad-libitum manner, i.e. with a feeling of freedom; ritards are appropriate at various places in these passages.

Q. What is the most important element in the interpretation of any piece of music?

A. The most important element in any piece of music is variety. We may have a series of passages that involve eighth or sixteenth notes, ascending and descending. Much will be gained by applying a crescendo as we ascend and a diminuendo as we descend. We may introduce some rubato. The following example from a Mozart sonata will illustrate this principle:

An interesting way to create a very strong expressive accent is to play a particular note before it is due if that note falls on a strong beat. You might say that we slightly anticipate that important note. I like to refer to that as "porte." Here is an interesting example of that:

Porte Anticipate   Vivaldi, Concerto in A Minor

Q. Would this anticipation upset ensemble playing?

A. It could if it is not done properly. The soloist would play the note slightly before it is due, and the piano or orchestra will play the note exactly on time.

Q. How can we apply the principle of variety in the use of dynamics?

A. Within each dynamic level, whether it is pianissimo or fortissimo we are permitted to make crescendi and diminuendi, and still remain within the orbit of the particular dynamic level.

A passage in fortissimo must not be played so that every note is fortissimo. If it is an extended passage, we must learn to play creatively with dynamic variety. For example, if we have a long passage marked pianissimo, it would not be interesting to play every note at the same dynamic level. There must be slight crescendi and diminuendi throughout the passage. Reiterated notes will also have to be colored by slight changes in dynamics. This will apply to every dynamic level.

Performers will often play louder immediately when they see the word "crescendo." When you see that word, do nothing. Think. Plan the crescendo very scientifically. Each note, if possible should be played a little louder than the preceeding note. If two to three notes on a short crescendo are played exactly alike, we are actually spoiling the gradual development of that crescendo.

Q. How about the long crescendo?

A. Long crescendi must be worked out carefully. We cannot keep getting louder and louder when it is an extended crescendo. That may be tonally and physically impossible. The entire passage may include some slight diminuendi, but the total effect should be one of a gradual crescendo.

Q. What suggestions have you for playing a crescendo on a long note such as a half note or a whole note?

A. Mentally divide the half note into eighth notes, and play each eighth note a little louder. Divide the whole note into quarter notes and do the same. It would be the reverse in a diminuendo.

Q. What creative approach can you suggest to lead to a fermata?

A. There are several ways to approach a fermata. You may make a crescendo or a diminuendo, with or without an accelerando. You may also make a slight ritard. This will depend on the emotional content of the passage.

Q. If we study the principles of interpretation, would that tend to make our performance rather stilted?

A. No. Actually, studying these principles should help the performer play with originality. In actual performance, however, the application of these principles should not seem obviously contrived. A performer must have such a complete mastery of the technical skills and interpretive formulae that the audience will not be aware of their use. The performer must have freedom, and at times give the illusion of spontaneity and improvisation.

But the one thought that I consider of paramount importance is that the performer must feel the emotional content of each phrase. We cannot expect the audience to feel the emotional message if the performer fails in the sublime duty to the composer to serve as an interpreter.

Q. How can we train students to play musically?

A. The first thing we have to do is to teach the player to think vocally while playing a melodic passage. A player should think vocally even when performing rapid movements, such as the final movements of the Mozart sonatas or quartets.

To a great extent, our duty is to phrase in the same manner in which one breathes. There is a relationship between the two that must be carefully cultivated. The essence of it all is musical punctuation, as though singing a song. The vocal comma should be applied much more in the performance of string music.

More attention should be devoted to actual phrasing. After all principles of phrasing and interpretation are planned, science ends and art begins.

How and When to Practice

Q. When is the best time of the day to practice?

A. If you are referring to young students, that decision should be made by both the students and the parents. Often parents make the mistake of asking students to practice when they are engaged in other activities. Practice sessions, if possible, should be scheduled a day, or even a week, in advance. When students agree to set aside certain times for practice, they are more likely to practice willingly. Interrupting students when they are doing something that is pleasurable may not be the best way to develop a love for the instrument and a desire to practice.

You must also realize that when pupils leave school, they are entitled to some outdoor play. On the other hand, once they become involved in an outdoor activity, it is difficult for them to start a practice period.

Q. In your many talks with parents, when do they feel is the best time of the day to practice?

A. Either before or after dinner or just before bedtime. Then there is the question of homework, religious training and other activities. It all has to be very carefully worked out.

Q. What should a student play to start a practice period?

A. When they are still in an elementary method book, the session should start with that book. As a rule, the method books include scales, some technical exercises, and pieces, which will represent a balanced program

Q. What about the advanced player?

A. There are many opinions. Many artists feel that a practice period should start with a slow movement, or long bows, using détaché and martelé bowings. Many feel that starting with scales is not necessarily the best way to begin.

Some students do not look forward to practicing, but once they get started they enjoy it. That is why, at times, starting with a piece may be very practical. It is not essential that practice periods start always with scales, and certainly they should never begin with music that is very rapid.

Q. How involved should parents be in the actual practice session?

A. Often students do not enjoy practicing because it is a lonesome experience. A parent may say to a child, "Please, go upstairs to your room, close the door, and practice."

For many students that is not a pleasant prospect. All students like to feel that their parents are interested in their music, and many will enjoy their parents' company while they are practicing.

However, there are certain dangers. Since carelessness and errors are inevitable, parents may get into the habit of constantly scolding. The student may then associate practicing with a displeased parent. Practice sessions should be a pleasant experience to be enjoyed by the student and the parent.

While parents may not know very much about music, they can help by gently suggesting certain things that can always be improved: posture, concentration, tone quality, and intonation. The parent should not, however, assume the role of the teacher and correct every mistake.

Another danger is that parents are too frequently interrupted by such things as phone calls, etc.

Practice sessions should include as much approval as possible, with a minimum of criticism. Goethe said, "Encouragement after censure is as the sun after a shower."

If possible, practice sessions should be inspiring. There is always something praiseworthy about a performance of a student, even though there is much that may be criticized. Every time a criticism is made a child's spirits fall. Every time there is praise, the spirits rise.

Q. Isn't it advisable for a student to have some practice time alone?

A. Yes. It will prevent complete dependency on the parent.

Q. At what age are children likely to enjoy practicing alone?

A. From my own experience, and after speaking with many great artists I would say that between the ages of 12 and 14, students are likely to take a greater interest in their practicing and will start to enjoy practicing alone.

Q. Should students be urged or occasionally forced to practice?

A. All the great artists with whom I have spoken to said they had to be reminded or urged to practice. Otherwise they would not have achieved their technical skills.

Q. What suggestions have you to improving the quality of practicing?

A. The student should first play the music straight through and mark each measure that presents certain difficulties.

Q. What might some of these difficulties be?

A. They might be a particular shift, a particular rhythm, poor tone quality on one or more notes, touching two strings instead of just one, or any other technical problem. After that, the student should be taught to identify the problem and then to analyze it. If it is a shift, it should be isolated and practiced slowly in different tempos.

But that is not all. Students must play difficult passages in different ways, in different bowings, such as martelé, spiccato, etc., or in different parts of the bow. The idea is to develop more technic than is absolutely required to master that particular passage. Then start one measure before each difficult passage and play to a measure beyond it in order to develop continuity of performance.

Students must realize that every error is imprinted on the subconscious mind. Difficult passages must be played correctly a few times in order to erase the incorrect impression that was previously made. When students realize the importance of repetition and how much it will improve their playing, they will be more likely to enjoy playing difficult passages many times.

Q. How long should they practice?

A. A very young child who has been studying the instrument only three or four months cannot possibly practice an hour a day. Two 10-minute periods might be enough at the very beginning, then it may be three 10-minute periods or two 15-minute periods, then two 20-minute periods.

Q. Repeating passages many times requires patience. How can we teach students to be patient?

A. Patience is a sensation that students must memorize. If we suggest that patience is a challenge, and that they will grow up to be fine human beings if they learn to become patient, it may be all the motivation that they will need.

We might ask them to play a slow scale, holding each note for four beats. We then challenge their patience by asking them to hold each note for five counts, then for six counts, then for eight counts, taking a breath at the beginning of each note.

Q. Isn't it natural for a player to take a breath before a long note?

A. No. It must be cultivated and practiced just as relaxing the entire body must be learned and practiced.

How to Avoid Nervousness in Public Performance

Q. How can we teach performers to understand the principles of relaxation?

A. We really cannot. They must experience two extremes before they can understand the process of relaxing specific muscles. They must first learn how to tense muscles and tighten them until the muscles become rigid and immobile. Then, as they gradually release the tension, they can understand what relaxation really is.

For example, if I ask you to make a fist and tighten it as much as possible, the entire arm will be rigid. If you then gradually open the fist, you will be memorizing the sensation of the difference between tension and relaxation.

Q. What are some of the causes of the trembling bow?

A. One of the manifestations of nervousness is a trembling bow, particularly around the middle of the bow. It is important to determine the cause of the trembling. It could be a lack of bow technic, or it could be the result of nervousness.

If it is due to a lack of bow technic, it can be helped by practicing the hand and finger stroke in different parts of the bow: the frog, the middle, six inches from the tip, and at the tip. Sometimes the difficulty might be traced to too much firmness in the way the bow is held or too little firmness. Each player must examine the bow hold to determine the possible cause of the trembling.

Q. What suggestions have you for avoiding the trembling around the middle third of the bow?

A. As we approach the middle, there must be a slight, gradual turning of the lower arm in the elbow joint in a rotary motion. When there is not enough of this rotary motion, the tone may become "surfacy." This might be the cause of the trembling in the middle third of the bow. Try applying a bit more upward pressure of the thumb against the frog.

Try lightening the pressure of the two middle fingers on the bow stick. Drawing whole bows while the two middle fingers are removed from the stick is an excellent exercise.

Q. What exercises can you offer to help relax the right arms?

A. Here are three exercises that can be performed <u>without</u> the bow:

Raise the bow arm as though playing on the D string. The elbow, the top of the hand, and the knuckle of the first finger should form a straight line. Place the tip of the right thumb in the first crease of the middle finger.

Exercise #1: In this position create continuous circles where the action starts in the shoulder joint. Relax the elbow and hand as much as possible while creating the circle. Do not raise the shoulder in the socket. Try to imagine that the arm is very light. Perform this motion in a clockwise and counterclockwise fashion. Time this with a metronome. For a complete circle at the shoulder set the metronome at 48.

Exercise #2: With the left hand grasp the right upper arm about three inches above the elbow joint. Hold the upper arm lightly, and create a continuous circle which comes from the elbow joint, clockwise and counterclockwise. Set the metronome at 60 for each circle.

Exercise #3: With the left hand grasp the lower right arm about three inches above the wrist. Create a circle with the right wrist, clockwise and counter-clockwise. Do this in a very relaxed manner. Set the metronome at 88.

In the first two exercises drop the hand slightly from the wrist joint. Decide which position makes you feel more relaxed. Continue the exercise daily in that position which relaxes you the most.

Q. In actual playing do we grip the bow a bit more firmly when we want a large sound?

A. Not necessarily. Try to produce as large a sound as you can with little or no tightening of the bow hold. This could be compared to the person who drives a car and grasps the wheel more firmly at faster speeds. This should not be done.

Here is an exercise to develop a flexible lower right arm. Again, without the use of the bow, raise the right arm to the height of the D string on the violin. Place the tip of the thumb in the first crease of the middle finger. With the first finger of the left hand, or with a dowel, gently push the lower right arm. Allow the lower arm to open and close as if playing four inches below the middle to as near the tip as possible. Try to feel as though the elbow will never stop opening and closing, as though it is thoroughly lubricated at the elbow joint.

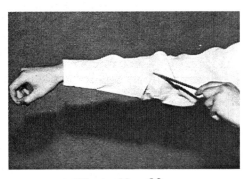

Photo No. 39

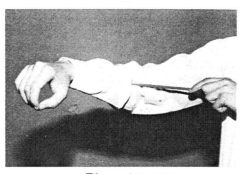

Photo No. 40

Q. What can we do to relax the upper arm?

A. Without the bow, imagine you are playing in the lower third of the bow. Set the entire arm in motion in the same way and allow the upper arm to feel that it is well lubricated in the shoulder joint. Do this about twenty times. In this way we memorize the sensation of a thoroughly relaxed and well-lubricated arm.

Q. Do you have any other exercises to relax the right arm?

A. Yes. Raise both arms to shoulder level as though you are ready to conduct an orchestra. Lower both arms slowly and gently until they reach chest level. In conducting we refer to this as the "ictus." At this point the orchestra starts. Lower the arms with precision to the level at the hips. Do not add more weight. Continue to do this a number of times. Now do the same thing, allowing the wrists to become extremely flexible so that as you raise the arms the wrists will droop gently. As you lower the arms, the wrists will come up. All of this should be done very gracefully.

Q. Are there any other suggestions to eliminate trembling of the bow?

A. The following is an exercise that you do with the bow and the instrument. Draw long bows, each stroke lasting eight counts on an open string. As you draw the bow raise and lower the right hand or wrist slightly in an undulating fashion with the bow remaining on the same string. Try not to interrupt the continuous sound. This will not only help to prevent trembling, but will develop more bow control.

Remember to use the full width of the hair above the middle of the bow. Going from one level to another should not be done with just the fingers, but with the hand from the wrist joint. Using less hair at the frog is helpful to prevent trembling.

Nervousness has a way of manifesting itself in the weakest part of a player's technic. That could affect the quality of one's public performance.

Q. I am sometimes fearful that I am going to miss a long shift. How can I avoid this feeling?

A. The slightest fear itself may cause you to miss a shift. Think positively. You must also learn to hear the note in your mind before you play it. This is basic.

You must have a kinesthetic sense of the fingerboard so that you know exactly where the note is. Shifting very slowly to that note is helpful in developing such a kinesthetic sense. You must memorize the sensation of the distance to that note.

Try to imagine that the fingerboard is indented where that note is to be played. Looking at the fingerboard is very helpful. This visual aid is of great importance.

Q. Does the way we hold the violin have an effect on nervousness in public performance?

A. Yes. The violinist (and violist) can be divided in to three categories: those who hold it too firmly with too much head pressure; those who hold it too loosely; and those who manage to place the violin or viola in such a way that they can balance the instrument with a minimum of head pressure and without tension in the left hand. This latter group avoids side pressure of the thumb against the neck and uses a minimum of downward pressure of the other fingers.

The violin is a very light instrument and the head weighs ten pounds, more or less. So, it certainly is unnecessary to provide additional head pressure which might lead to tension. Anything that leads to tension is detrimental in public performance. One must constantly experiment with the way one holds the violin. Elsewhere in this book we talk about the different ways to hold the instrument. It was Fritz Kreisler who told me that he held the violin in such a way that he applied a minimum of head pressure and sometimes no pressure at all. When he played passages that did not require shifting, he actually lifted his head from the chin rest.

The manner in which we place the fingers upon the strings is important. With some players, striking the strings at the very tips of the fingers is sometimes detrimental, not only to tone production but to a free left hand. It is better to experiment with the way we place the fingers, both in rapid and slow passages. Using more of the pad of the fingers is advisable in slow passages with or without vibrato.

Q. Do you have any specific exercises to avoid tension in the left hand?

A. The left thumb should be placed and shaped so there is great freedom of motion. In the Best of Sevcik, Vol 2, every other page is devoted to shifting studies. These studies might be practiced in two ways: 1) with the thumb in contact with the neck, and 2) with the thumb not touching the neck.

We must learn to shift with no contact between the thumb and the neck. Repeat this exercise with the thumb lightly contacting the neck. This procedure was recommended by Sevcik.

Many players exert too much finger pressure on the strings. When shifts are performed, ascending and descending, there should be only a feather weight pressure on the string during the slide. The hand and the entire left arm should be able to go from one position to another with the greatest of ease and a feeling of freedom. The fingers and the left wrist joint should be very flexible. Tension in the wrist joint may be responsible for tension in the left hand. There should also be great freedom in the left elbow. The entire left arm should be free from the shoulder joint down to the fingertips.

Q. What do we do if the fingers tremble and are not sufficiently under control for public performance?

A. Prior to going on stage many artists place their fingers in warm water until the trembling stops.

Q. In our practicing, how much time or effort should be devoted to looking at the bow when we play long notes?

A. It is wise to practice very long notes of different lengths while looking at a point on the fingerboard about an inch below the bow contact with the string. We should not, however, rely exclusively on this eye contact.

As we have already said, the same is true for long shifts. Look at the fingerboard to help memorize the exact distance of the shift. Long shifts should be practiced in two ways: 1) looking at the fingerboard, and 2) with the eyes closed.

Q. Is it possible for the vibrato to be affected by nervousness?

A. The vibrato can be greatly affected. The excitement of a public performance, coupled with a very fast vibrato, can spoil an otherwise good performance. Every so often during a performance the player must eliminate the vibrato on certain notes. It will not do any harm, and may actually prevent trembling.

From my experience in working with gifted children from the age of 4 years and older, I have noticed that they play in public without fear. They develop velocity and accuracy at an early age. One manifestation of great talent is the skill and ease with which they memorize . Sometimes students who are talented have only to play a composition a few times before they can play it from memory. They are likely to be a bit careless about changes of bowing and other details, but that can be corrected.

After a certain age (about 13 or 14), they may begin to become self-conscious. This may produce a certain fear at which point students must be carefully encouraged by their teacher.

Young people should spend many years developing long sustained tones in two different categories: 1) the even tone in all parts of the bow and at all dynamic levels; 2) The different types of tone color that they get from crescendi and diminuendi that are well coordinated with the various lanes. This must also include the technic of creating détaché and martelé accents on the up-bow and the down-bow. This means drawing the bow rapidly at the beginning of a stroke and immediately slowing the speed of the bow. There is a whole series of skills that comes under the heading of ACCENTS. (refer to Chapter 12)

Q. How do you feel about exercises that involve eurhythmics?

A. I am heartily in favor of them. I also feel that the teacher should create a series of tension and relaxation exercises. Arm movements that are used by ballet dancers are very effective in developing a sensory awareness of the graceful and relaxed relationship between the upper arm, lower arm, and the hand and fingers.

Here is a good exercise that relaxes the back muscles which affect one's playing. Stand erect, but in a relaxed manner, feet 12 inches apart, weight equally distributed between the feet. Let the arms hang loosely at the sides. Rotate the body from the hips in an oscillating motion. As the body moves allow the arms to swing in a semi-cicular motion, still hanging loosely at the sides. Do this for two minutes.

Now clench the fists tightly and tense the arms from the shoulders down to the hand. Continue to allow the arms, now tightened, to swing, but for no longer than 20 seconds.

Q. Is it necessary to do several of the cycles in order to memorize the difference between the tension and the relaxation?

A. Yes. Perform three cycles. Each cycle should consist of two minutes of relaxed swinging, 20 seconds of tensed swinging, and another two minutes of relaxed swinging. If possible, do this three times a day.

Q. How should one breathe while doing this exercise?

A. Breathe normally during the relaxed portion. During the tensed portion, inhale for the first ten seconds and exhale during the second ten seconds. Pucker your lips while exhaling in order to prevent the sudden release of air.

Q. If one has a fear of memory lapse when playing in public, what can you suggest to gain more confidence?

A. You must spend more time learning your work so that you have no doubt about the fact that you know it thoroughly first from the structual standpoint.

Let's take the first movement of a sonata or a concerto which most likely will be in sonata form. Examine the architecture of the movement. It may open with an introduction, which will be followed by the exposition of the themes.

Know when a theme begins and ends, and when a new theme starts. There may be a transitional phrase between these themes. Know when that transitional phrase starts and ends and when the new theme begins.

Know when the development starts. You must study the development in relation to the themes.

Then, we have the recapitulation. Here the themes are again presented and frequently with some slight differences. These differences must be thoroughly memorized.

The way the entire movement ends must be studied carefully.

Q. Should I then start memorizing the different themes?

A. Yes. But even before that you must divide the themes into various segments and phrases. With each phrase there is always one note that is of greater importance than the others. This is referred to as "the magnetized note." That is the note you are moving toward. In your performance the audience must become aware that you are approaching the "magnetized note."

When you memorize a phrase it is not enough to know just that phrase. You must also memorize the note that begins the following phrase. That note must always be memorized in conjunction with the previous phrase. Knowing that note will frequently come to your rescue if your memory fails. It makes good sense also to memorize separately the transitional phrases and how they connect to the following themes. When you have a sequence (e.g. two bars followed by another two bars) that sequence may be written higher or lower on the scale, or it may be an exact reproduction. The difference should be very carefully memorized.

Q. Should the notes be memorized before the dynamics are memorized?

A. It is a mistake to memorize notes and then add the dynamics. Each phrase must be memorized in conjunctiion with the emotional message within the realm of good musicianship.

Try to identify the emotional message of each phrase. What is the mood? Try to build up a large vocabulary of descriptive words, adjectives and adverbs. We know a phrase much more thoroughly when the emotional message is part of the concept. Write down the different words you can use to describe a theme.

Q. When I go on stage what is the thought that should be uppermost in my mind?

A. The emotional message of the work. Remember that you are an intermediary between the composer and the audience. You are to tell the audience what Beethoven means when you perform one of his sonatas. Thinking about yourself and the way you are going to play is not conducive to a good performance. Certainly the composer does not expect you to be thinking about yourself. Doing so would be a form of selfishness. When you play for an audience, you are to think only of the music.

A number of years ago, I was backstage with a young violinist who was about to make his New York debut at Carnegie Hall. His teacher was with us. This young man said to us, "I just wish tonight were over. I feel so nervous. I know I will feel better after I get started, but I wish I could get over the initial fright." His teacher replied in mock anger, "You are going out there to say something. If you think about anything else but the music, about the critic or anyone in the audience, you should pack up and go home. You must go out there with humility, but with pride, in bringing to the audience the message of the work you are going to play."

Q. What suggestions have you to test a player's memorization of a piece of music?

A. Here are some excellent tests:
1. the ability to play the music and be concerned only with the emotional message and not the notes;
2. the ability to start at any given point in the music, for instance, to play just the themes or just the transitional phrases;
3. the ability to write out the entire piece or sections of it — to save time the player could try to write just the first measure of each line or of just the themes.
4. the ability to see the printed page in one's mind;
5. the ability to play mentally the entire piece.

Q. How do you project the emotional meaning of a passage to the audience?

A. We learn to project emotional thoughts in two ways: The first is to experience the emotion as we play. The second way is to use corresponding body movements or body language.

Let us consider the first way — experiencing the emotion as we play. If you do not feel the emotion, the audience will not experience it. You have to understand the emotion and project it into your playing by first feeling it. The success of actors is determined by how intensely they can feel the emotion they are about to portray for the audience.

Now for the second way using corresponding body movements to indicate the emotion. This is not a superficial thought. It is an advanced technic. A beginner should be taught the proper use of body movements. One of the great violinists of our time suggested that we learn to replace one facial movement with another. He made a thorough study of most of his facial expressions. He uses his eyebrows, lips, and the turn of the head.

In a general way there are a number of emotions that you must know how to express: joy, depression, anger, agitation, anxiety, love, serenity, repose, frivolity, solemnity, passion, playfulness, etc.

Q. How about the technical side of the problem that will permit me to develop enough bow control to gain confidence for public performance?

A. You must develop enough bow control so that the audience will not be aware of any possible nervousness or tension on your part.

Q. What is the best exercise to start with in order to develop that bow control?

A. There are three excellent exercises:

1. Play long bows softly in the first or second lane for 60 seconds without any trembling of the bow and without any crescendo or diminuendo. Inhale as you start the stroke and again at the middle of the bow. Draw the bow lightly, withholding any of the weight of the arm or hand. On the up-bow you must not permit a crescendo as you approach the frog.

2. The 30-second stroke on two strings: here you must make sure that both strings sound simultaneously throughout the entire bow stroke. No crescendo or diminuendo! Breathing plays an important part in bow control. When you do this 30-second stroke on two strings, divide the bow into three parts. Play smoothly in three parts of the bow for ten seconds each. Spend more time practicing in the lower third of the bow. Concentrate on producing a beautiful sound throughout the entire bow stroke.

3. The third exercise is to develop another kind of control. That is the ability to play a note from 30 to 60 seconds with the bow being held one-half inch above the string. The object here is to prevent the bow from rising or falling. Try to maintain the distance of one-half inch above the string throughout the stroke. Many of the great artists continue to practice these three exercises throughout their careers.

Q. How often should these bowings be practiced?

A. If you have the time, try to spend one hour each day on these bowings. You do not have to do them every day, but only three or four times per week. For the average young student even ten to fifteen minutes a day will have some value.

Excellent studies can be found in the book, Etudes for Technic and Musicianship, particularly Vols. 2 and 3, and in a book entitled Orchestral Bowings. These should be started with students at a very early age.

Q. What other bowings can you think of to develop bow control and avoid the manifestations of nervousness?

A. The COLLÉ bowing in the following exercises will not only develop breadth of style, but will also help to control nervousness.

Play one note, collé, at the frog. (The collé is described in Chap. 9.) Play one down-bow at the frog, then lift the bow in a complete circle, and play the same note down-bow at the tip. That is, use the same collé stroke at the tip, this time using the full width of the hair. (So it is down-bow at the frog and down-bow at the tip.) The object of this exercise is to be able to place the bow at the tip without a tremor. The bow hair has to be set into the string without any trembling or extra bounces. The instant the hair is in contact with string, it is pressed firmly into the string straight down. Repeat this a few times at the frog and the tip, all down-bows.

Standing on your toes during this exercise is also helpful because it develops balance. Keep breathing.

Now do it at the frog and at the tip in up-bows. Motivate students to take pride in the way they hold the instrument and draw the bow. They should be praised when they develop good posture in performance. Good posture that brings balance between the two arms represents a poise that is very beneficial. Poise is a form of self-confidence.

The next way to do it is down-bow at the frog and then up-bow at the tip. Then up-bow at the frog and down-bow at the tip.

It is certainly a worthwhile exercise and it will benefit anyone who applies it. Spend ten or fifteen minutes with this bowing several times a week.

Q. What is the difference between nervousness and excitement?

A. Excitement is frequently mistaken for nervousness. Excitement is necessary for a vital performance. The difference is this. When a performer is nervous, the bow is likely to tremble. Vibrato is affected, and the entire left arm may become very tense. The right arm may lack freedom of motion, and the quality of tone may suffer because the bow is drawn in the wrong lane.

Excitement is a positive force in the sense that it adds interest and vitality to the performance. Positive thinking is a growth process which should be nurtured gently by the teacher. So much of one's life is controlled by one's thinking that we can actually change our lives by altering our thoughts. Confidence should be built up throughout the student's formative years. Everything that a teacher tells a student is extremely vital. It can breakdown or build up a child's confidence.

If performers would go on stage with the intention of sincerely enjoying their own playing, they would be less susceptible to nervousness.

Q. Are there drugs that can aid in conquering nervousness?

A. There are drugs that some performers use. They relieve only the symptoms of nervousness, and should be used only in extreme circumstances and always under the guidance of a physician.

Q. What specific breathing exercises can you offer to help control the manifestations of nervousness?

A. I consider this extremely important because nervousness does affect breathing. Many players have not been taught how to breathe. Here is a technic that will help to develop this skill:

Take your pulse when you are reasonably calm. Inhale to the count of six in the same tempo as your pulse rate. Hold that breath to the count of six and exhale to the count of six, still counting at the rate of the pulse. Training yourself to breathe in a steady rhythm will help you to retain muscular control.

Q. How should we apply breathing during performance?

A. Singers breathe in accordance with the musical phrase. String players must do the same thing. We must inhale before we start a phrase, and we must inhale during the phrase.

Q. When do we exhale?

A. Do not worry about exhaling. This is a natural process because of the physical activity. It is on the inhaling that we must concentrate our efforts.

Many string players clench their teeth while playing. This should be avoided. When playing, the lips may touch lightly or even separate slightly. The upper teeth should never touch the lower teeth. Here are three basic bowing exercises where skillful breathing is to be applied.

Exercise #1: Developing an even tone. Play a long open string note for twelve counts. ($\quad$ = MM 66) Inhale for four counts. Hold the breath for four counts. Exhale for the last four counts. Do not make a crescendo or a diminuendo throughout the bow stroke. Do this in the following dynamics: pianissimo, piano, mezzo piano, mezzo forte, forte and fortissimo. Memorize the sensation of how much additional bow weight is required to produce an even tone after the middle of the down-bow is reached.

Exercise #2: Developing a long crescendo on the down-bow and a long diminuendo on the up-bow. Inhale, hold, and exhale as in exercise #1. Increase the bow weight as the bow is drawn down-bow. Decrease the bow weight as it is drawn up-bow.

Exercise #3: Developing a crescendo-diminuendo within the same bow stroke. The breathing technic is the same as in exercises #1 and #2. The height of the crescendo should occur exactly in the middle of the bow.

In these three exercises much thought should be given to the gradual changing of the lanes and bow speed as the bow is drawn.

Q. Do physical calisthenics have any bearing on avoiding nervousness in public performance?

A. They are very important. Daily calisthenics and even some slight stretching exercises before going on stage are very valuable.

Here are some exercises you might do before going on stage:

1. Head Massage —

   (a) Forehead Massage. Using the middle fingers, massage the areas directly above the eyes for 30 seconds in a clockwise motion, and then for 30 seconds in a counterclockwise motion.

   (b) Back of the Head Massage. Massage the back of the head in areas that are directly behind and on the same level as the areas described in the Forehead Massage.

Photo No. 41   **Photo No. 42**

(c) Massage the areas under the cheek bones and directly under the eyes.

(d) Same exercise in the back of the head.

Photo No. 43

Photo No. 44

2. Mouth Exercise —
   Pretend to chew a large wad of chewing gum. Exaggerate the motion. Create circles with the lower jaw. This prevents the clenching of the teeth.

3. Neck Massage —
   (a) Massage both sides of the larynx.   (b) Same exercise on the back of the neck.

Photo No. 45

Photo No. 46

4 Neck Rolls —
   (a) Create a series of circles, clockwise and counterclockwise, letting the head roll from shoulder to shoulder.
   (b) Write out the alphabet in the air, pretending the tip of the nose is a pencil. Use large motions.

5. Shoulder Shrug —
   Create a series of circles by raising and lowering the shoulders clockwise and counterclockwise.

How to Develop Confidence in Upper-Position Technique

A positive mental approach is necessary to develop confidence in the performance of passages in the high positions. Too much time is spent thinking about left-hand technique in terms of positions in numerical order. The positions then become compartmentalized in our minds.

While a working knowledge of each position is essential, we must begin to think about the fingerboard as a single unit. This will help us develop a kinesthetic sense of the entire fingerboard. We must also get away from the thought that the second, fourth, and sixth positions are more difficult than the first, third, and fifth. It is valuable to adopt the Sevcik theory, which is to develop technical skills in the first position and then to apply these same skills in each of the high positions.

From the standpoint of beautiful tone production, the following must be considered: the higher the position, the firmer the left-hand finger pressure, the lighter the bow pressure, and the closer the bow must be to the bridge.

1. ESTABLISHING THE FRAME OF THE LEFT HAND (the distance between the first and the fourth fingers)

Play a one-octave scale on one string with left-hand pizzicato. In addition, practice the following exercises five different ways:
a. whole bow martelé;
b. two and four notes to a bow, legato in quarter notes;
c. four eighth notes to a bow;
d. dotted eighths and sixteenths — four to a bow;
e. sixteenths and dotted eighths — four to a bow.

G string

G string

2. PLAYING A TWO-OCTAVE SCALE ON A SINGLE STRING WITH THE SAME FINGER

Starting with the open string, we play a two-octave scale with the first finger. We do the same, starting with the open string, first finger, and then completing the scale with the second finger. Continue this process with the third and fourth fingers. The exercise should be done in the minor keys and in broken thirds on all strings.

153

3. TWO-OCTAVE SCALES IN ONE POSITION

As soon as possible, students should play two-octave scales in the same position, starting with the first finger and going all the way to the fourth finger on the highest string. The scale is to descend after playing the highest note twice. Continue playing two-octave scales, each a half step higher, and starting each scale with the first finger. Continue until you reach the tenth position, note C and the G string.

4. MATCHING TONE STUDY

Play F natural with the first finger on the E string. Play the same F with the second finger on the A string in the fourth position. Play it with the third finger on the D string in the seventh position, and then with fourth finger on the G string in the tenth position. Then go back to the third finger on the D string, the second finger on the A string, and the first finger on the E string.

Start on F sharp and go through the same procedure, matching the notes on the other strings. Then start with G on the E string. Keep going up a half step at a time until you get to C on the E string, which will be in the fifth position. In this exercise you will cover almost every note on the fingerboard. Practice these in quarter notes, two and four to a bow, then in dotted eighths and sixteenths, four to a bow, and finally in sixteenths and dotted eighths, four to a bow.

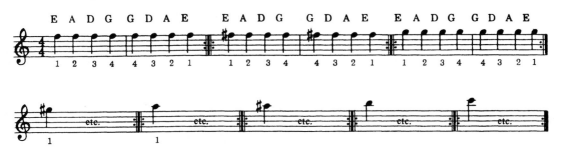

5. OCTAVE STUDY WITH VARIOUS FINGER PATTERNS

Play the finger pattern four times. Then, without a pause, play the same pattern an octave higher on the same string, and then back down again to the lower octave, four times in each position. Start a note higher with the first finger, note G in the second position. Play it four times, then play it an octave higher and then down again. Keep going up to the seventh degree of the scale, which will be the note E. This should be practiced on all strings in the upper half of the bow and in the lower half, starting down-bow and then up-bow.

This study is valuable for the following reasons: It encourages the development of the fast down-bow and the fast up-bow. It develops left hand finger action and clarity in the various positions. It develops good intonation in the various positions. It develops correct bow contact with the string in the various positions. In the higher octaves it may be necessary for a finger to leave the string in order to play the next higher note:

6. DEVELOPING A KINESTHETIC SENSE OF THE FINGERBOARD
(Finding the same note immediately)

On the piano or any other instrument, play any note between the open D string and second finger on the E string. The student should try to find this note on the violin on the G string, but not slide into it. Place the third finger above the string and let it drop right on the note. Then strike another note and do the same thing. Do this many times.

The notes struck on the piano should include sharped and flatted notes. If this is practiced faithfully, a "sixth sense" will soon develop, and when the student hears a note the finger will immediately drop on it without having to slide into it.

Play any note between the two notes in measures (a), (b), (c) and find it on the string designated above.

7. A TWO-OCTAVE SCALE ON A SINGLE STRING WITH DIFFERENT FINGERS

Practice this on all strings in various bowings and rhythms. Practice each set of fingerings a few times before going to the next set.

on the G string

8. ONE-OCTAVE SCALES IN DOUBLE STOPS

Practice the following scales in thirds, sixths, octaves, and tenths, using whole bow martelé in separate quarter notes, then legato quarter notes two and four to a bow, then eighth notes, sixteenth notes, dotted eighths and sixteenths, and sixteenths and dotted eighths.

Start the one-octave scales from the first position, then from the second position, then from the third position, and finally from the fourth position.

Practice these in major and minor keys.

8a. A ONE-OCTAVE SCALE IN THIRDS ON THE SAME TWO STRINGS USING THE SAME TWO FINGERS

Notice that one finger may move a whole step and the other finger may move a half step on any particular shift.

Practice both fingerings.

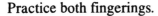

A one-octave scale in thirds on the same two strings using different fingers.

8b. A ONE-OCTAVE SCALE IN SIXTHS ON THE SAME TWO STRINGS USING THE SAME TWO FINGERS

As in Exercise 8a, notice that one finger may move a whole step and the other finger may move a half step on any particular shift.

Practice both fingerings.

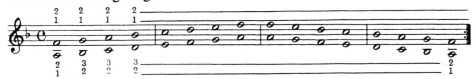
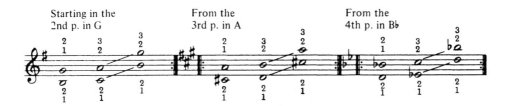

A one-octave scale in sixths on the same two strings using different fingers.

8c. A ONE-OCTAVE SCALE IN OCTAVES ON THE SAME TWO STRINGS USING THE SAME TWO FINGERS

Practice both fingerings.

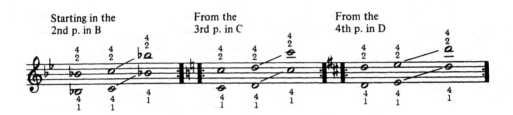

A one-octave scale in fingered octaves on the same two strings using different fingers.

8d. A ONE-OCTAVE SCALE IN TENTHS ON THE SAME TWO STRINGS

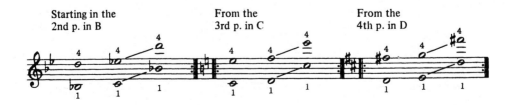

9. LOCATING ALL THE HARMONICS ON EACH STRING

Finding each harmonic will help to develop a greater sense of security over the entire fingerboard. It is also valuable for bow control.

Practice them détaché, whole bow, upper half and lower half, spiccato near the frog, repeating each note two and four times.

Practice finding them on all the strings, using both fingerings.

This example is on the G string.

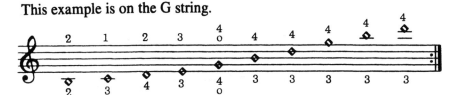

Repeat the above finger pattern on the other strings.

10. FINDING THE OCTAVE WITH A SINGLE FINGER ON THE SAME STRING

Practice this also with the second finger ascending and descending, then with the third finger, and finally with the fourth finger.

Practice this octave study slowly, then gradually more rapidly.

11. VARIOUS INTERVALS ON THE SAME STRING

(eighths, ninths, tenths, elevenths, twelfths on one string)

Practice this in major and minor.

Practice this with the lower fingering and then with the upper fingering.

Practice this on all strings in ⁵⁄₄ time. This exercise should also be practiced starting from B flat and B natural in the second position, and from C in the third position.

12. TWO-OCTAVE MAJOR AND MINOR ARPEGGIOS ON THE SAME STRING

Practice the following arpeggios on all strings, three and six notes to a bow. In the seventh and ninth positions the first finger must remain down on the string. Practice these in martelé, spiccato, and various mixed bowings — also staccato, three and six notes to a bow, starting up-bow and down-bow. Practice both fingerings.

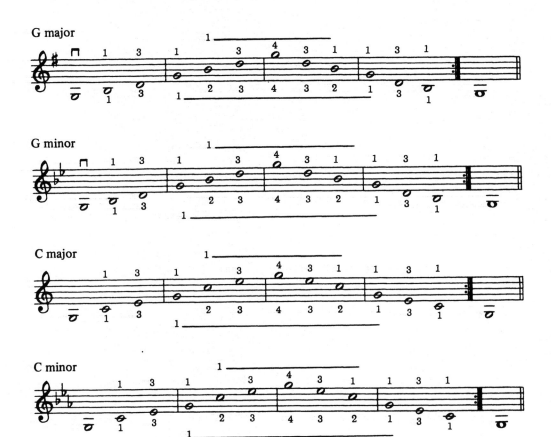

Rote Exercises to Develop Specific Skills

We Memorize the Sensations of Different Finger Pressures

Place the third finger on G in the first position. Press the finger firmly into the string. Now flatten the third finger a bit, and touch the string as lightly as possible. The note you will hear is called a harmonic, and will sound two octaves higher. Do the same with the fourth finger. The diamond-shaped note is the harmonic. Do this on all strings. This is what it will look like in print.

When playing artificial harmonics practice a few times pressing the higher finger firmly on the string, then a few times placing the higher finger lightly on the string. This will help to develop a kinesthetic sense that will be helpful for intonation.

Artificial harmonics should be practiced where (1) the first and fourth fingers represent an interval or distance of a perfect fourth, (2) the first and fourth fingers represent an interval of a perfect fifth, (3) the first and third fingers represent an interval of a minor third.

When playing artificial haromonics practice a few times pressing the higher finger firmly on the string, then a few times placing the higher finger lightly on the string. This will help to develop a kinesthetic sense that will be helpful for intonation.

Shifting

When you shift from the first to the third position, first hear the note in your mind, then test it with the open string. During the sliding you must lighten the finger pressure on the string, and relax the thumb pressure on the neck.

Shifts are always made with the entire hand, the thumb moving with the finger. On the downward shift the thumb leads the way.

The Matching Tone Game

Practice the following rote game first slowly, then playing a bit faster. The notes must sound exactly the same. Repeat each measure four times. Practice this on all strings.

We Prepare for Advanced Playing by Developing Left-Thumb Technic

Play a harmonic by placing the 4th finger very lightly on the G string in the 1st position.

Now slide the 4th finger up on the G string until it reaches the harmonic an octave above. This will be about two inches from the end of the fingerboard. The thumb starts to go under the neck immediately and continues until the tip of the thumb touches the end of the neck, where it joins the body of the instrument. The cushion of the thumb touches the neck during the slide. Never squeeze the first joint of the thumb against the side of the neck.

■ EXERCISES USING THE GEMINIANI CHORD

Place the first finger on E (F), the second on A (C), the third on D (G) and the fourth on G (D). While keeping the fingers down, stand on your toes and play four pizzicato notes on each string. Repeat this line three times.

Our Fingers of the Left Hand Become Much Stronger

Place the fingers in the Geminiani chord. Raise and lower the first finger eight times in quarter notes, keeping the other fingers down.

Do the same with the second, third, and fourth fingers, keeping the other fingers down. As time goes on, you may do this in eighth notes for as many beats as you can without tiring too much.

We Widen Our Span of Concentration with Different Finger Pressures

Place your fingers in the Geminiani chord. Stand on your toes and hold the violin as high as the upper lip. Press the first finger firmly into the string while the other fingers remain on the strings very lightly.

Concentrate on the firm pressure of the first finger to the count of ten. Repeat this with each finger. Try to imagine that the fingerboard is made of rubber and that the object is to sink the finger into it.

We Develop Different Finger Speeds

Practice the Geminiani Chord without the bow, in a very slow tempo, but lifting each finger rapidly and replacing it slowly.

We Develop Left-Hand Finger Coordination

To develop the ability to place two fingers on the strings simultaneously, practice double stops in the following manner as a variation to the Geminiani Chord exercises. This is done without the bow, and then with the bow, in separate bows, two to a bow and four to a bow, and also in dotted eighths and sixteenths.

Do this on all strings. Create additional exercises similar to this.

Instant Memory

The teacher will play a phrase twice, as the pupils relax and listen. The teacher will then play the phrase a third time, a bit softer and slower. Now it is played a fourth time even slower and softer as the pupils listen with closed eyes. (Some pupils may require two or three additional renditions of the phrase.) The pupils will sing the phrase once or twice and then attempt to play it.

On the last note (a half note) we will ask the pupils to tap lightly on the floor twice with their right foot as they hold this note.

This game of "Instant Memory" should be played regularly. The phrases should become very gradually more difficult, to make sure that each experience is, to a great extent, a success experience.

Tapping of the foot may or may not be included in later games of "Instant Memory."

■ HOW TO DEVELOP A WELL-SHAPED LEFT HAND

We Test and Shape Our Left Hand

To make sure of a well-shaped left hand mark a spot on the fingerboard where the fourth finger should be placed. Place the 4th finger down on the A string and allow it to remain down. Place the 1st finger on the D string. With the 1st and 4th fingers REMAINING on the strings, count to ten. Do this twice. Practice this for many weeks.

We Continue to Develop a Well-Shaped Left Hand

Place the first two fingers on the D string. Allow them to remain on the D string while you play the open A string. Do this a few times. Now do the same thing with the third finger.

We Frame a Scale for a Well-Shaped Left Hand

Play the following scale slowly in separate bows. The open strings should be heard continuously throughout each quarter note. Memorize this scale-frame and play it four times each day.

This next exercise is a bit harder.

Play open D for four slow counts. On the second beat, while holding the open D, pluck the open G three times with the fourth finger. Repeat this using the first finger, second and third fingers. Do this on all strings.

We Start to Develop a Good Trill

Repeat each section four times without a pause, using the entire bow. Gradually play them faster and faster. When you play in a slow tempo, work the fingers very hard, lifting them rather high in a curved shaped from the base joints. As you gradually get faster keep the fingers closer to the strings. Practice this on all strings fortissimo, then pianissimo.

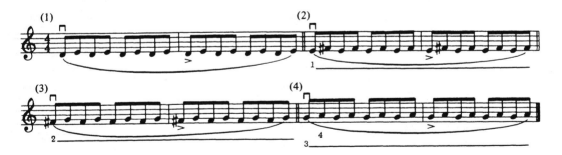

We Develop Brilliance by Quick Left-Hand Finger Action

Lift the finger quickly from the string as you play the small notes. These are called mordents. Accent each quarter note and leave a clean stop before starting the next mordent. Play scales in this manner.

We Learn How to Apply Head Pressure on the Violin

a. Holding the violin in LEFT-HAND OPEN STRING position, press the head lightly on the chin-rest. Photo 47A. Count four. Throw the head backward as far as you can. Photo 47B. Press backward firmly to the count of four. Do this exercise a number of times.

b. Repeat the exercise but now do it to the count of two.

c. Repeat this exercise to the count of one.

Photo No. 47A

Photo No. 47B

The Head Pressure Exercise in Different Rhythms

The teacher will play the following rhythms as the pupils hum, sing, or clap.

Place the head on the chin-rest. The head is then to leave the chin-rest. Now press the head back as far as possible. Then down again.

This is to be done a number of times in the following rhythms. Do each group a few times.

Photo No. 48

We Strengthen Our Shoulder and Neck Muscles

Hold the violin without the aid of the left arm. As you do this, cross your arms over your chest. Bend the knees slightly, then straighten up. Do this four times.

Photo No. 49

A Game to Make the Left Arm Strong

Place the palm of the right hand on the muscle of the left arm as shown in Photo 49. Bear down on the muscle of the left arm while the arm resists this force by pressing upward. Do this to the count of six, then rest the count of six. Repeat this exercise four times.

■ **WALKING GAMES**

Place the bow on the D string in the center. Draw the bow eight times, leaving a slight pause between each stroke. Take a slight breath after the fourth time with the bow remaining on the string. As you do this, walk slowly in a large circle. The violins and violas will do this while the cellos and basses remain in the center of the circle. Take a step for each bow stroke. We may also walk in a large square instead of a circle.

A Straight Line Formation

We will divide the class into two lines, with the pupils facing each other. Draw the bow four times, walking toward each other, with a slight pause between each note. Take a breath, then again draw the bow four times with each group walking backwards away from each other. Do this a few times on each string.

We Walk as We Play Scales

Play a major scale starting on the G string, the D string, and the A string in the following ways, very slowly, each note twice:
a. walking in a square formation.
b. walking in a circle.
c. free walking.
d. the class facing each other, walking toward each other, and then walking backwards.

Walking and Breathing Using the First Finger

In this Rote Game, we alternate between the 1st finger on the D string and the 1st finger on the A string. This is what it will look like when it is written.

| walk slowly | stop – take a breath | walk slowly | stop – take a breath | walk slowly | stop – take a breath | walk slowly |

We Learn to Find Notes Quickly While We "Tap, Tap, Tap."

When you see this sign (♩) remove your fingers from the string and tap the top of the violin quite firmly with the second finger. Do this in quarter notes. Use the fleshy pad of the finger rather than the very tip. Play one-octave major scales in C, G, and F in the following manner — ascending and descending.

We Strengthen the 4th Finger — Left Hand Pizzicato

Place the first, second and third fingers down on the D string. Now place the fourth finger down about an inch from the third finger. Remove the three lower fingers. Pluck the D string with the fourth finger. Do this eight times, but do not move the left elbow or the left thumb as you pluck the open string.

More Left-Hand Pizzicato

Pluck the open string four times with the fourth finger. Place the first finger on the string and pluck the firsst finger with the fourth finger. Now place the second finger a full step away from the first finger and pick this with the 4th finger. Do this on all strings.

Pluck open G and D with the 4th finger of the left hand in slow quarter notes as follows:

While this pizzicato finger pattern goes on, another group will play *Mary Had A Little Lamb* on the G string.

Reverse the groups. Now pick open D and A while *Mary Had a Little Lamb* is played on the D string.

We Play *Mary Had A Little Lamb* — Left Hand Pizzicato
(We Continue to Strengthen Our 4th Finger)

Play *Mary Had A Little Lamb*, picking each note with the 4th finger of the left hand. Press the fingers quite firmly. This is what it will look like in the music.

Left-Hand Finger Action From the Base Knuckles

In this Rote Game we memorize the sensation of finger action which originates in the base knuckles. This is done without the violin. With the left arm up as though holding the violin, curl the fingers into the palm of the hand. Photo 50A. Now bring the finger tips up as in Photo 50B pressing them firmly into the base knuckles, do this four times; take a breath; do it four times again; then take another breath. Do this sixteen times altogether.

Photo No. 50A

Photo No. 50B

We Continue to Memorize the Sensation of Correct Finger Action

Photo No. 51

This Rote Game will help us make sure that the fingers strike and leave the string from the base knuckles. Lift your left arm as though you are holding the violin. The finger nail of the first finger must face directly at you.

Strike the tip of your thumb with the tip of the first finger, snapping it back very quickly. Do this six times with each finger. Use only the very tip of the finger, making sure that it snaps back in a curved shape. The finger action must come only from the base knuckle as the Photo 51 where the 2nd finger is used.

We Continue to Strengthen Left-Hand Fingers

A successful way to strengthen the fingers of the left hand is to press the fingertips against the fleshy part of the thumb, midway between the tip and the first joint. Do this with each finger individually and then all four fingers together. Another valuable exercise is to press the fingertips against the under side of a table or chair. Do this in quarter notes or eighth notes.

■ LEFT-HAND FINGER FLEXIBILITY

The Scissor Spread to Develop Finger Flexibility

Photo No. 52

With the help of the thumb and the first finger of the right hand, spread apart the first finger and the second finger of the left hand as far as possible. Hold the fingers apart to the count of six.

Repeat this four times. Do the same with the other fingers. Photo 52.

We Develop Flexible Fingers of the Left Hand

Tie a rubber band around the four fingers of the left hand, near the tips. (Photo 53) Hold the left hand up as though you are playing. Stretch the first finger as far away from the other three fingers as you can. Hold it there to the count of six.

Now stretch the fourth finger, moving it away as far as possible from the first, second and third fingers. Hold this to the count of six.

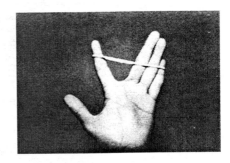

Photo No. 53

We Develop Flexibility of the First Finger

Place the three fingers down on the A string in a 2-3 finger pattern. Lift the first finger and place it on the D string, but allow the second and third fingers to REMAIN on the A string.

Slide the first finger from its regular position to as far back to the nut as you can. Do this sliding up and back eight times in slow quarter notes. You are now developing flexibility of the first finger. However, you must make sure that the second and third fingers REMAIN down on the A string. Try not to move the left thumb during this slide.

We Memorize the Sensation of Finger Independence

Place the 4th finger down on the E string. Leave it there. Try not to move it. With the 4th finger remaining down, play *Mary Had a Little Lamb*, starting with the 2nd finger sharped on the D string.

■ ELEMENTARY COUNTING GAMES

A Counting Game with Left-Hand Pizzicato

Pluck each open string eight times. Take a breath. Now pluck each open string six times and take a breath. Pluck each open string four times. Take a short breath. Then do it three times and finally two times, taking a short breath between each group.

A Counting Game in Half Notes (In Three Parts)

a. The teacher will play a D-major scale in half notes on any instrument. The class will count out loud "one-two" for each note.

b. The teacher will play a G-major scale while the class counts "one," and taps the right foot on the floor for "two."

c. The class is to play the D-major scale and the G-major scale, tapping on the floor for the second beat of each half note.

A Counting Game in Dotted Half Notes

The teacher will play a D-major scale in dotted half notes while the class will count out loud — 1-2-3 for each note.

The teacher will play a D-major scale while the class will say "one" for the first beat of each note and tap lightly with the right foot on the floor for the second and third beats of each note.

The class will now play a D-major scale in dotted half notes, walking slowly, taking three steps for each note. The walking is to be free in different directions for each dotted half note. The scale is to be played above the middle of the bow, and then repeated playing below the middle of the bow, very lightly.

We Develop an Orderly Mind

We are going to play a one-octave G-major scale in $\frac{4}{4}$ time, starting on the G string in slow quarter notes. Each measure will contain a quarter rest, and for the remaining beats we will repeat each note three times. On each rest, we will tap lightly on the floor, or we will call out "rest." Keep the bow on the string during the rest.

a) The rest will occur on the 1st beat. b) The rest will occur on the 2nd beat. c) The rest will occur on the 3rd beat. d) The rest will occur on the 4th beat.

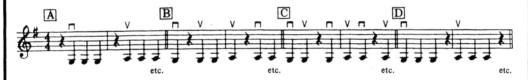

Vary the Rote Game by playing scales starting on the D and A strings. This music-mental gymnastic is challenging and difficult at first.

We Learn How to Start a Bow Stroke

In this Rote Game we will memorize the sensation of allowing the hair of the bow to sink into the strings. We will learn just how much pressure is required to draw a clear tone. Place a piece of adhesive tape or draw a chalk mark at the center of the bow. Do the same thing midway between the middle and tip of the bow and midway between the middle and the frog.

a. Place the middle of the bow on the D string.

b. Pinch the bow so that the hair is firmly pressed into the string. The stick must be directly above the hair.

c. With the hair firmly pressed into the string, move the string laterally side to side or from right to left. The object is to do this motion without sounding the string. This will not be easy. Do this a few times from right to left.

d. After you have done this a few times lift the bow about six inches from the string — then replace it on the string and repeat the right to left motion. Do this on all strings.

e. Now repeat this Rote Game higher up on the bow where we placed the mark (midway between the middle and tip of the bow). Do this on all strings.

f. Now let us repeat this Rote Game but, this time we pinch the bow on two strings at the same time, as for example: the G and D, D and A, etc. **We always place the bow down on the string from above. We never bring the bow up to the violin.**

We Memorize the Sensation of Different Tone Colors

Play *Mary Had a Little Lamb* on each of the four strings. Ask the class which tone color they prefer. Our object is to have them become cognizant of different tone colors. Now divide the class into two groups, each group getting into a different corner of the room. One group will play *Mary Had a Little Lamb* on the G string and the other on the D string. Now have one group play it on the D string and the second group play it on the A string.

We Develop a Flexible Right Wrist

To develop flexibility of the right wrist without using the instrument, practice space writing. Hold the right arm as though playing on the D string. Move the right wrist, keeping the arm motionless, in clockwise and counterclockwise motion, pausing for an instant at each imaginary hour. Write the entire alphabet in the air. Write a paragraph from a book in mid-air using only the hand.

We Develop Finger Flexibility of the Right Hand

Hold the bow in front of you as you see in Photo 54. Crawl with the fingers up and down the entire stick without touching the hair. Do this quite slowly. As you do this take a deep breath at the frog, at the middle, and at the tip of the bow.

Photo No. 54

We Memorize the Sensation of Different String Levels

Place the middle of the bow on the G string. Pinch the bow hair into the string, moving the string side to side without making a sound. The right elbow should form a straight line with the top of the hand or wrist. It should also form a square. Do this a number of times on each string. On the E string, the elbow should be about three inches from the body.

Right-Arm Magic to Develop Flexibility and to Find String Levels.

At the frog, play the G string, using about ½ inch of bow. Then stop. Now proceed quickly to the E string without touching the middle strings. Stop. Now go back to the G string. Do this 4 times in 3 places: at the frog, at the middle, and at the tip. On the G string, the right elbow should be as high as the bow and on a straight line with the top of the hand. On the E string, the right elbow should be about 3 inches from the side.

We Memorize the Sensation of Finger Action for String Changing

Place the bow on the E string at the frog, with the right thumb bent outward, and the little finger will be curved. The right elbow should be about three or four inches from the body forming a straight line with the top of the hand. Raise only the fingers until the bow touches the A string. Go back to the E string by lowering the fingers. Do this six times without moving the elbow or arm. Practice this on all strings.

How to Develop a Smooth Bow Change at the Frog

Start playing up-bow at the tip on the G string. When you are three inches from the frog, stop and allow the wrist and fingers to complete the stroke. Stop again. Now start down-bow with the arm taking the initiative. The wrist and fingers will not start the down-bow stroke. Later on start practicing it without stopping, with the wrist and fingers helping you to go smoothly from one bow stroke to another. Practice this on all strings.

We Memorize a Different Sensation of Bow Weight

Hold the bow on the stick six inches from the frog. In this bow position play a D-major scale in quarter notes, each note four times. Play this scale above the middle of the bow using the full width of the hair, with the stick above the hair. Do not allow the stick to tilt towards the scroll. Memorize the sensation of transferring the weight of the right hand to the first finger.

■ BOW CONTROL

Play scales, each note smoothly on the down-bow, but lift the bow at the tip about two inches above the string. Replace the bow on the string, starting the up-bow with a firm, clear sound.

To develop a highly sensitive right forefinger, learn to play whole bows counting eight slow beats with the first finger raised slightly from the stick.

The Right-Hand Telescope (We Check Our Bow Hold)

Play a D-major scale in half notes, with a half rest following each note. During the rest, move the entire arm in a complete circle back to the frog. Before starting the next note, look through the circle between the thumb and the first finger as you would through a telescope. The object is to see that the thumb is curved outward and that the the little finger is curved to its fullest extent. Practice the Rote Game again, holding the bow with only the thumb and fourth finger.

We Learn to Play Pizzicato

Place the tip of the right thumb on the end of the fingerboard underneath the E string. With the thumb set, pluck the string with the first finger of the right hand about 1¼ inches from the end of the fingerboard. Pluck the string with the fleshy part of the first finger near the tip. Photo 54.

A Pizzicato Rote Game in Three Parts

a. Play *Au Claire De La Lune* pizzicato starting on the D string.

b. Half the class will play it arco and the other half will play it pizzicato, simultaneously.

c. Half of the class will play one phrase "pizzicato" (two measures). When they have finished the phrase, the rest of the class will play the second phrase "arco." Continue in this manner. Photo 55.

Photo No. 55

We Develop Bow Control Using the Col Legno Stroke

COL LEGNO means to strike the string with the stick of the bow, which should face the player. Play a D-major scale striking each note four times. We will play this scale five times, each time in a different spot on the string. We will refer to these spots as lanes.

Here are the five lanes: 1. At the fingerboard. 2. Near the fingerboard. 3. In the center, between the bridge and the fingerboard. 4. Near the bridge. 5. At the bridge, as close to it as possible.

For a new effect, ask half the class to play the scale in a natural manner while the other half plays it *col legno.* Then change around.

To Bow Straight We Learn to Use the Lower Arm

In this Rote Game we memorize the sensation of using only the lower arm from the elbow joint. Draw the bow through a napkin holder as in Photo 56.

Draw the bow from the middle to as near the tip as possible over the left shoulder. Play this Rote Game in slow quarter notes, making sure that the upper arm does not move.

Photo No. 56

We Learn to Use the Whole Bow

When we use the whole bow we start at the frog with the RIGHT THUMB BENT OUTWARD, and the LITTLE FINGER CURVED TO THE FULLEST EXTENT. When we get to the middle we will call out "change," and then will use the full width of the hair with the stick directly above the hair. On the up-bow we start with the full width of the hair, and when we get to the middle we call "change," and turn the bow to the side with the stick tilted slightly toward the scroll. When we get to the frog the little finger and the thumb again must be curved.

Play a D-major scale in half notes, each note twice, using the whole bow. On the second beat of each half note the whole class will call out "change" at exactly the same time. The tone must remain continuous.

We Develop Freedom in Our Bowing

Play a D-major scale in half notes, using the entire bow. After each half note introduce a half rest. Lift the bow high above the head during the rest, and bring the bow down in the form of a circle for the next note.

Start each note with the weight of the body on the left foot. For the second beat of the half note, transfer the entire weight of the body to the right foot in a swaying motion.

During the half rest as the bow is being brought up in a circle, transfer the weight to the left foot, ready to start the next note. Take a deep breath during the half rest.

Sway from left foot to right foot   Transfer weight to left foot   Continue in the same manner

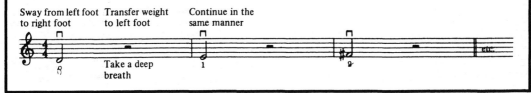

Take a deep breath

We Memorize the Sensation of Opening and Closing the Lower Arm

The hand is placed in the middle of the bow on the stick, then slides down to frog and back again to middle. Here the right elbow is too low. It should be on a level with the hand. (Photo 57A) Then the hand slides down to the frog. (Photo 57B)

Photo No. 57A

Photo No. 57B

We Develop More Freedom in the Bow Arm

In this Rote Game we go quickly from "arco" to right-hand pizzicato. Play a two-octave G-major scale in the following manner:

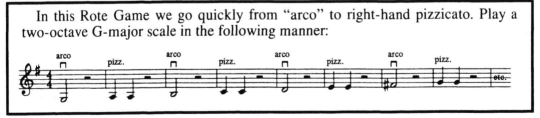

The Bow Retake (More Bow Control)

Start at the frog and play to the middle. Lift the bow quickly, and, in a circular motion, bring the bow back to the frog, to start down-bow with the side of the hair on the next note.

We Memorize the Sensation of Different Bow Speeds

Play one-octave scales in separate bows — C, G, D, F — using a whole bow for each note. Hold the first note for one count, the second note for two counts, the third note for three counts, and so forth. Continue in this manner up to eight beats, and then down to one beat. Here is the pattern: 1, 2, 3, 4, 5, 6, 7, 8, 7, 6, 5, 4, 3, 2, 1.

It will be lots of fun to play scales holding each note for the duration of the numbers in any of the pupil's phone numbers. An 0 in the phone number means rest for one count.

We Develop Good Posture and Relaxation with Body Motion

Play a D-major scale holding each note eight beats. Stand on your toes and move your body slowly in the direction of the bow. On the down-bow move to the right, on the up-bow move to the left. Take a slight breath as you start each bow stroke.

We Develop Muscular Poise and Freedom in Our Bow Arm

Play a G-major scale in the following manner: Play the whole note in the 4th lane, near the bridge, and the quarter note in the 2nd lane, near the fingerboard. For the whole note, maintain fortissimo throughout, even at the tip. For the fast quarter note, use the whole bow, but do not allow the bow to quiver, and be sure to remain in the 2nd lane.

Play this scale once through, starting down-bow and once through starting up-bow.

The Two-Lane Scale — To Produce a Beautiful Tone

Play a G-major scale in quarter notes, each note four times. Play the first four notes forte in the middle lane. Now play the next four notes piano in the second lane. As you practice this you will become more skillful in going from one lane to another.

Another Two-Lane Scale to Develop a Beautiful Sound

Play the first note piano in the second lane, and the second note forte in the center lane. Use the whole bow for each note. Lift the bow after the second note, during the quarter rest. Practice the scales of C, G, D, F, and B flat in this manner.

The "Scoop a Tip" — To Develop Bow Arm Strength

Place the tip of the bow in the second lane, with the full width of the hair on the D string. Transfer the full weight of the hand to the first finger. Press the bow into the string firmly and create a martelé attack by lifting the bow quickly in a scooping motion, until the tip points to the ceiling.

We Develop Flexibility and Relieve Stiffness of the Bow Arm

Play a C-major scale, holding each note for four slow counts. As you hold each note, roll the bow stick between your fingers, which means that the bow stick will tilt first towards the fingerboard, and then towards the bridge.

Make sure that the fingers do the rolling in the hand. The tone must be continuous. This alternate tilting should be done first in quarter notes, then in slow eighth notes.

We are Going to Develop a Big Tone

Place the bow down at the frog, pinching the bow into the string. Draw the bow quickly and firmly to six inches from the tip, but do not release any of the bow pressure on the string. Rather add more pressure after you pass the middle.

Lift the bow and go back to the frog as quickly as possible, making a complete circle with the arm. Pinch the bow again and repeat. Play a D-major scale in half notes in this manner. Start each note in the second lane (near the fingerboard), and sustain each note in the fourth lane (near the bridge).

For Tone Control, We Coordinate Breathing and Bowing

Play an F-major scale forte, holding each note eight counts. Take a deep breath on the first beat of each note. On the fifth beat take a slight breath but do not allow the bow to tremble. If it does, apply a slight upward pressure of the thumb against the frog. You also might try relaxing the second and third fingers or even lifting the second or third finger, from the bow stick.

For additional bow control, divide the bow into four equal parts. Play whole notes (andante) moving the bow quite quickly in the first quarter, slower in the second and third quarters, and quite quickly in the fourth quarter. Play scales in this manner.

Coordination for Fast Trills

To develop bow and left-hand finger coordination during a fast frill, exercises similar to the following will encourage a quick lifting of the fingers and a smooth bow change.

This should be practiced at the frog and at the tip.

We Develop a Lighter Bow Arm

To develop control and lightness of the bow arm (at all levels of proficiency practice slurred arpeggios in the lower half of the bow.

Practice all bowings on open strings, then with natural harmonics (detaché, martelé, spiccato, sautille, riccochet, collé).

We Develop Various Bowing Styles

Play one-octave Major and Minor Scales in the following manner: Practice near the frog using the spiccato bowing.

We Play Three-String Chords with Body Motion for Greater Freedom

Play the two lower notes at the frog near the fingerboard, using about two inches of bow. Go immediately to the two upper notes, playing them near the bridge. As you play the two upper notes, move your head and your body quickly to the left.

How to Play on Three Strings at the Same Time

Set the bow firmly into the middle string of the chord about an inch from the frog. Draw the bow quickly and release this pressure at the same time, using about five and one-half inches of bow. Lift the bow, and in a quick, circular motion draw the bow back to the frog and play the next chord. As you play each chord, move your head and body quickly to the left.

Exercises to Develop Double-Trills

Each of the following measures are to be played using the variants above. The entire exercise is on the G string and D string.

To help strengthen the left hand, practice these while lifting the lower fingers from the strings.

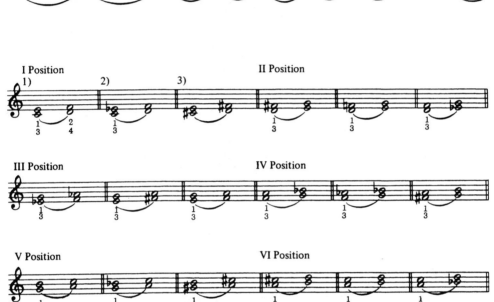

Thoughts to Ponder
(with exercises)

Vibrato

To develop a rich, warm vibrato consider adopting the following procedures:

1. Practice any scale, holding each note for five seconds, then four seconds, then three seconds, then two, and then one second.
2. Vibrate by oscillating five times to the five-second note, then five times to the four-second note, then five times to the three-second note, then five times to the two-second note, then five times to the one-second note.

Eventually, oscillate approximately five times to each note that is one second in duration. That may well be considered a good speed for the development of a fine vibrato.

Neglected Notes

Here, we have a series of notes that are likely to be neglected on a string instrument during a performance:

1. the note after a three- or four-voice chord that is played very loudly;
2. in groups of four sixteenth notes the fourth note is likely to be neglected;
3. in rapid détaché passages that involve triplets, the second note of each triplet is often neglected;
4. in arpeggios that involve triplets on three strings, the first note of every other triplet is apt to be neglected because it occurs on the up-bow;
5. in a four string arpeggio which involves four notes, it is the second of each group that is apt to be neglected;
6. the note before a shift and the note after the shift;
7. there is a tendency to neglect using vibrato on significant notes that are played with the fourth finger; it may be advisable to use more of the fleshy pad while not allowing the first knuckle of the fourth finger to collapse;
8. if we play a series of notes in one down-bow, the notes closer to the tip tend to be neglected and may lack the quality of brilliance because of lack of bow weight;
9. in détaché passages, the first and last notes of various rhythmic groups are frequently neglected; (to counteract that tendency, practice passage similar to the following, accenting the notes that are marked);

10. There are two occasions when notes must be held for their full value because there is a tendency to shorten them slightly.
    a. before a string change or skipping of strings,
    b. before a shift.

Interpretation

- Ask students to sing or hum all phrases, where possible. This will aid in identifyng the various phrases and in understanding the emotional message.
- In the performance of a work, logic must prevail, but there must be contrasts so that there is freedom within unity. A great artist must know how to handle restrictions. In the interpretation of works by Beethoven, there are more guidelines than with other composers, particularly Mozart. However, within these guidelines, there are greater restrictions, but the need for freedom is also greater.

The Left Thumb

Here, I would like to summarize the action of the left thumb when going from the first to the fifth positions or from the third to the fifth positions.

The thumb is moved back (toward the scroll) along the neck, parallel to the G string. While this motion is made, the first finger knuckle moves away from the neck. This will bring the knuckles of all four fingers parallel to the strings. It permits the hand to move in a straight line when the shift is made. At the moment the shift is made, the thumb moves forward until the tip (or a quarter-inch from the very tip) of the thumb is in contact with the curve of the neck. For players with normal hands very little additional movement of the thumb is necessary for the fingers to move up to the very high positions. In the following example, the thumb should go back while the knuckle moves out on the note G to prepare for the shift to the note, B.

Shifting

● Experiment by slowing the bow speed and lessening the finger pressure on the string during a long shift to permit a precise and clean change of position.

● As you ascend to a higher position the thumb, in a circular manner, gradually arrives at the curve of the neck. The point that I would like to make is that the thumb, in descending, may not assume its normal position until it reaches the third position.

Bow Planning

● Good bow planning is valuable for a good musical performance. It prevents the non-musical stressing of notes that are not important. Good bow planning makes possible the stressing of notes that *are* important.

● Good bow planning is deciding how to divide the bow and how much bow should be used for notes of equal or unequal length, and should be a constant part of one's practice. Artistic playing requires rational distribution of the bow for every phrase.

● Find out which part of the bow in which you are least comfortable. Spend some time improving your technic in that part of the bow.

Bow Control

● For additional bow control, divide the bow into four equal parts. Play whole notes (andante) moving the bow quite quickly in the first quarter, slower in the second and third quarters, and quite quickly in the fourth quarter. Play scales in this manner.

● Marking various parts of the bow with tape provides a very helpful visual aid for the student. Students should be able to play in every part of the bow with accuracy. Mark the bow in half (one marker), in quarters (three markers). At other times mark the bow in thirds (two markers). As students advance, more and smaller segments may be marked for greater control and subtlety.

● To play lightly in the lower half of the bow, lessen the upward pressure of the thumb.

● Play scales, each note smoothly on the down-bow, but lift the bow at the tip about two inches above the string. Replace the bow on the string, starting the up-bow with a firm, clear sound.

● Many players place the tip of the right thumb about a quarter inch or half inch from the edge of the frog. They feel that there is an advantage in controlling the bow weight when they play at the tip.

The Little Finger of the Right Hand

To make sure that the little finger of the right hand remains close to the third finger on the bow, place a piece of adhesive tape on the bow stick (double-thickness) about ¾" from the third finger. This will prevent the little finger from sliding down towards the screw. It will also be easier to keep the little finger well curved.

Flexibility of the Right Hand

- To develop flexibility of the right wrist without using the instrument, practice space writing. Hold the right arm as though playing on the D string. Move the right wrist, keeping the arm motionless, in clockwise and counter-clockwise motion, pausing for an instant at each imaginary hour. Write the entire alphabet in the air.
- Write a paragraph from a book in mid-air.

Developing A Straight Bow

- To help beginners develop a straight bow, place a white narrow strip of adhesive tape to the instrument under the strings, midway between the bridge and the fingerboard (middle lane).
- Another visual aid to develop a straight bow is to mark a spot on the wall and ask the pupil to align the screw of the bow with that mark.
- A good exercise for developing a straight bow is as follows:
  Draw a whole bow, down-bow, while your eyes are closed. When at the tip, open your eyes. Is the bow parallel to the bridge? Do the same on the up-bow. If you can draw a straight bow with your eyes closed you are making fine progress in developing a good bow arm.

Changing Strings Smoothly

- Arpeggios that ascend are a bit more difficult to bow smoothly than arpeggios that descend.

The lower fingering permits the player to play two notes on each string. The right arm will now drop at a similar rate of speed. If the open strings are used instead of the fourth finger, the bow would have to drop very quickly from the G string to the A string and much more slowly from the A string to the E string. During this quick dropping of the right arm, there is some danger of slighting the one note on the D string, note E.

- We must learn to go from one string to another in every part of the bow. Smooth string changes should be practiced at the frog, near the frog, at the middle, slightly above and below the middle, near the tip and at the tip.
- Try to avoid changing strings on a half-step. In the following example the upper fingering is preferable:

Try to avoid crossing to an open string when the note below the open string is a half-step. In the following example the upper fingering is preferable:

The Hooked Bowing

The hooked bowing is excellent to develop muscular control of the bow arm. Practice this bowing below the middle of the bow, using the hand and fingers as well as the entire arm in one well coordinated motion. Above the middle, of course, more bow weight must be applied, but using the lower arm instead of the whole arm.

The Up-Bow Staccato Below the Middle

If you wish to develop a good up-bow staccato below the middle of the bow, practice it on two adjacent strings as a double-stop. As an example, place the first finger on the D string, note E, and fourth finger on the A string, note E. Then play a fast tremolo, stiffening the arm slightly. Move the arm slowly in a horizontal manner, starting above the middle and going to about four inches below the middle.

The Ricochet Bowing

To develop a more colorful ricochet, experiment by dropping the bow on the string from different heights.

The Sautillé Bowing

- Passages that use sautillé bowing should first be practiced on the string, above the middle of the bow, at the middle, and below the middle, using only the hand (wrist) and fingers.
- For a louder and slower sautillé bowing, play a bit closer to the frog and use slightly more bow hair. Use more forearm and less wrist motion.

Practicing

- As a general rule, practice many difficult passages slowly and close to the frog.
- Rapid passages should be practiced many times slowly and then gradually faster. It will be helpful to practice these passages backward (in reverse) and with different styles of bowing. This may be applied to scales, i.e. starting from the highest note.
- If you have only a few minutes to practice on a particular day, concentrate on a passage in which you are deficient. It might be a passage in tenths, a glissando, or a beautiful tone with vibrato on some very high notes on the highest string or on the lowest string.
- Aim for efficiency during practice periods. Pinpoint the difficulties and focus your attention in improving them.

- Daytime practice periods should be used for slow practicing and analytical work to develop mastery of technical difficulties. However, the evening should be devoted to the repertoire to be played in concert style, playing very intensely and imagining that an audience is present. The evening might well be devoted to memorizing the repertoire.
- Everything one practices at home must be technically and emotionally transferable to a public performance.

Left-Hand Finger Independence

To develop finger independence compose many passages similar to the following:

Trills

- Trills on low-pitched strings may be performed a bit more slowly than trills on high-pitched strings. Low-pitched strings vibrate quite a bit more slowly.
- While playing whole-tone trills, when the note above the principal note is a major second higher, do not allow the whole step to gradually diminish. When playing half tone trills where the note above the principal note is a minor second, do not allow the half step to gradually grow wider.

Octaves and Tenths

While playing octaves and tenths, remove the second and third fingers from the string. However, when playing fingered octaves, do not remove the first and third fingers when playing the second and fourth fingers. When playing tenths, remove the second and third fingers.

Widening the Web Between the Finger of the Left Hand

Practicing exercises similar to the following will be very helpful (keeping the first finger down on the string):

Stage Fright

- Much nervousness is caused by fear of the stage. We can overcome much of that fear by practicing on an empty stage.
- Stage fright is the fear of difficult passages and loss of memory. Choose music beneath the level of your technical ability. Mentally play the first line of that music many times. A good beginning is of great importance. Self-confidence comes to your aid after the first line. One concert artist recommended smiling constantly before going on stage. Smile to everyone back stage. Smile to yourself. Remember that the audience is your friend. Treat them that way.

Memory

- To improve your ability to memorize try memorizing a short piece, phrase by phrase, away from the instrument.
- To improve your memory write on a pad the words or proper names that you are apt to forget, and review them frequently. Write them in alphabetical order.
- Teachers whose pupils may perform poorly on occasion and concertizing artists who may receive a bad review must learn how to forget. The past has no reality except in the mind. We must develop the ability to forget. Constantly remembering unpleasant experiences saps one's energy. Knowing how to forget is often helpful in strengthening one's memory. The discipline required to forget is similar to that required to develop a good memory.

How to Sit When We Play

Sit on the edge of the chair, more to the right. If you look down to your left you should be able to see some of the chair. The left foot should be in front of the chair, firmly set on the floor. The right knee should be slightly lower and a bit to the rear. The right lower leg should practically touch the right leg of the chair. This will give greater freedom in bowing. Try to sit in such a way that the bow will travel over the right knee.

Relaxation

- A proven exercise of great value to prevent nervousness and to aid in relaxation is as follows:
  1. sit up straight in a chair that is not too soft;
  2. relax by closing your eyes and letting all your muscles go limp;

3. yawn gently two or three times; if you cannot yawn, lower your jaw and create circles, clockwise and counterclockwise about ten times in each direction;
4. concentrate on your breathing; each time you exhale, say to yourself a phrase of three or four words which is meaningless, or a single word, such as "sun".

Practice this exercise before each public performance and twice a day, ten minutes each time.

- Too many players are likely to raise the right shoulder slightly as they approach the frog. Practice long notes and try to relax the neck and shoulder muscles as the frog is approached.

Right-Hand Pizzicato

In playing right-hand pizzicato in very rapid passages we may use the index finger and the middle finger alternately. But in extremely rapid pizzicato passsages we may only press the string in an up and down motion rather than actually plucking the string laterally. If open strings occur during such passages they might be plucked with the left hand.

Left-Hand Pizzicato

It is helpful in left-hand pizzicato to hold the left elbow further to the left than in ordinary playing. The finger producing a left-hand pizzicato should be moved slightly to the right on the violin and viola as it leaves the string.

Note Identification

- To read the high ledger lines rapidly, start from the third ledger line above the staff, which is note E. Consider this E as the first line in the treble clef and start counting up from that line. In your mind eliminate the first two ledger lines.
- Some students may be aided in developing reading skills if they are reminded that in the first and third positions on the violin and viola the first and third fingers are line notes, and the second and fourth fingers are on space notes.
- In the second position it is just the opposite.

Intonation

- A good ear training exercise is to play with the first finger on the A string, note B, and the open E string. The same note B may have to be lowered slightly to play in tune with the open D string. Create exercises similar to this.
- Correct intonation does not always depend on the relationship to the neighboring finger. In double stops this relationship is essential. Most times, it is from the first finger that the other fingers automatically measure their distances. When shifting or leaping to a higher position (to a 2nd, 3rd, or 4th finger), it is frequently beneficial to place the 1st finger simultaneously for greater security.
- To determine when strings are false, check each pair of adjoining strings for perfect 5ths when a finger is placed on them simultaneously. Do this, not only in the 1st and 3rd positions, but in the 5th and 7th positions as well. The 1st and 2nd fingers should be used.

Inspiration and Motivation

*A teacher who is attempting to teach
without inspiring the pupil with a
desire to learn is hammering on cold iron.*

Horace Mann

Q. What is it that teachers must inspire students to do?

A. Teachers should inspire students to:
1. enjoy practicing;
2. practice thoughtfully and analytically;
3. become involved in the emotional message of each phrase.

There often seems to be a closed door that prevents a pupil from becoming emotionally involved in the music. A teacher must inspire the pupil to remove any barrier that will prevent that emotional involvement.

Q. How can we help pupils to become emotionally involved in the music?

A. Much can be done by suggestion:
1. a pupil must know exactly what the emotional message is; once the teacher describes the emotion, it will most likely remain with the pupil permanently;
2. the student should develop a very large vocabulary of descriptive words; this will result in an increase of the different emotions which the student will try to convey musically;
3. pupils must learn to become emotionally and interpretively very flexible; for example, within any sixteen bars we may have three or four different emotions: forcefulness, tenderness, capriciousness, etc.

Q. From the technical standpoint have you any suggestions to help the pupil properly project the various emotions?

A. The teacher should:
1. prescribe exercises using very fast whole bows which are to be played with good tone quality;
2. encourage the pupil to identify the magnetized or most important notes in each phrase;
3. insist that the pupil observe the accents, both written and unwritten. Accents are the very essence of emotionial expression.

Q. To what extent should body motion be involved in performance?

A. Body motion is important from the standpoint of emotional involvement in performance. However, it can be disturbing if it does not reflect a genuine emotional expression. The same can be true of facial expressions.

Q. Would you consider this a major reason for attending live performances?

A. I am glad you brought that up. Inspiration is fired by listening to and seeing other players who are inspired. Concert going is an essential part of a student's development.

Q. In a few words, what is the most important attribute which will make for a great teacher?

A. Will Durant, when asked what he thought was the most important word in the English language from the standpoint of human relationships answered "KINDNESS".

Somerset Maughm was asked the same question. He said that he could think of only one word which would say so much — KINDNESS.

Along with kindness there are three more attributes which are necessary to become a great teacher:
1. patience,
2. enthusiasm,
3. dedication.

This reminds me of a young student who had the courage to say to an impatient teacher, "Please, don't be impatient with me. God isn't finished with me yet."

From the standpoint of the teacher, wisdom is the ability to create alternatives. No week should go by without the teacher creating different ways to present the same material or skills. Music and art should not continue to be educational "minors." They should unquestionably be equated with the scientific areas of human experience and relationships.

It has been demonstrated that where there is a cleavage between the intellectual and the aesthetic development, we do not have a total human being. It is our role as instrumental teachers to create a better world through music.

If a teacher tells a student that a certain melody is beautiful, the student is more likely to consider it to be beautiful. There are certain abstract qualities that can be taught. It is important that students learn to differentiate between the things that are in good taste and the things that are not in good taste. It is possible to learn this at a very early age. It is the privilege of the teacher to develop a fine aesthetic awareness.

As teachers we must realize that every time we speak we are creating an influence in the lives of our pupils. We do not know when that influence begins or ends, but we do know one thing: it is very powerful.

Cello Supplement
The Basics —
Two Versions

Holding the Cello Bow

1. Hold the bow with the left hand, the hair facing the floor. Photo 58.

2. Bend the right thumb and place the right side of the tip of the thumb on the edge of the frog so that ⅔'s of the tip of the thumb will be on the frog and ⅓ will be on the stick itself. Photos 59A and B.

Photo No. 58

Photo No. 59A

Photo No. 59B

3. Put the first finger under the stick in the first joint—Photo 60. Carefully study the placement of the 2nd and 3rd fingers. Notice that they are placed loosely together, in a relaxed manner and are not spread apart. This applies also to the little finger.

4. When the bow is held in playing position the 4th finger should be perpendicular so that the four knuckles are directly above the stick.

5. Place the tip of the little finger so that it will cover the pearl piece on the frog. Notice the placement of the 2nd and 3rd fingers.

6. Hook the first finger under the stick in the first joint. Photo 60.

Photo No. 60

Holding the Cello

1. Try to obtain a flat-bottom chair.

2. Sit on the front half of the chair with the body straight and slightly forward. Both feet should be flat on the floor as though ready to stand, with the knees low enough so as not to obstruct the bowing. Photo 61.

3. Sit erect with the small of the back not curved outward, but rather slightly curved inward.

4. The tips of the toes should be about 20 or 24 inches apart depending upon the size of the pupil.

5. The upper part of the body should feel free, but make sure that the heels and toes are touching the floor, with the right foot forward about six inches.

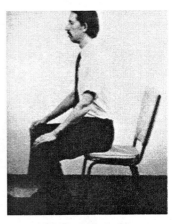

Photo No. 61

6. The cello should be tilted slightly from the left to the right in order to make playing on the A string more comfortable. However, the cello may be gently rotated to favor the lower strings if necessary. Notice the bow at the tip — Photo 63 and at the frog. Photo 64.

7. The end pin should be set in such a way that the scroll of the cello should just clear the player's left shoulder, about an inch from the player's neck. The adjustment of the end pin will vary according to the length of the player's arms. The longer the arms the lower the end pin.

Photo No. 62

Photo No. 63

Photo No. 64

The corner of the lower bout will contact the inner side of the thigh from three to five inches from the left knee cap. Photo 65. The right knee will brace the lower side of the instrument. Photo 66.

Photo No. 65

Photo No. 66

Placing the Fingers on the Cello

Study Photo 67. Notice that there is a circle between the thumb and the second finger.
Place all the fingers on the neck of the cello so that the first finger is about 2 ½ inches from the edge of the nut. The fingers should be slightly apart as seen in Photo 68.

Always make sure that the thumb is behind the neck and opposite the second finger. The thumb rests gently on the neck with practically no pressure, and it is possible for there to be a very slight curve of the thumb. It is safer if the thumb is actually straight. Photo 69.

The tip of the elbow should be practically at a straight line with the middle knuckle of the second finger, as in Photo 68.

Note that the first finger is practically at right angles to the string and that the other fingers are placed in a square manner with the finger tips on the fingerboard.

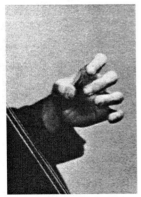

Photo No. 67   **Photo No. 68**   **Photo No. 69**

Holding and Drawing the Cello Bow
As Posed by Orlando Cole

1. Hold the bow with the left hand, the hair facing the floor. (Photo 70) The tip of the little finger should cover the pearl piece on the frog. Hook the first finger under the stick in the first joint. The second finger as well as the remaining fingers are placed loosely together in a relaxed manner, not spread apart.

2. Place the right side of the tip of the thumb on the edge of the frog so that a part of the thumb also touches the stick itself, with most of the thumb on the frog itself. We might say that ⅔ of the tip of the thumb will be on the frog and ⅓ on the stick itself. Make sure that the thumb is curved, particularly in the middle joint. (Photo 71)

3. When the bow is held in playing position the 4th finger should be perpendicular so that the four knuckles are directly above the stick. (Photo 72)

4. The bow is to be drawn at right angles to the string. Place the elbow gently on the string about 1 ½" below the end of the fingerboard at right angles to stroke with the whole arm from the shoulder. (Photo 73) Below the middle we start each stroke with the whole arm from the shoulder. As a general rule we introduce the lower arm independently from the upper arm at the elbow joint when we play from near the middle to the tip.

5. On the A and D strings the lower arm is used exclusively from about the middle to the tip. (Photo 74) On the two lower strings it is not necessary to introduce the lower arm until we have well-passed the middle of the bow going toward the tip. The important thing is to keep the bow traveling parallel to the bridge at all times.

Holding the Cello

1. The player sits at the edge of the chair with the body straight and slightly forward. (Photo 74)

2. Both feet are flat on the floor as though ready to stand, with the knees low enough so that the bowing will not be obstructed.

3. The end pin should be set in such a way that the scroll of the cello should just clear the player's left shoulder, about an inch from the player's neck. The adjustment of the end pin will vary according to the length of the player's arms. The longer the arms the lower the end pin.

4. The corner of the lower bout will contact the left knee. The right knee will brace the lower side of the instrument.

5. The cello should be tilted slightly from the left to the right in order to make playing on the A string more comfortable. However, the cello may be gently rotated to favor the lower strings if necessary.

Photo No. 70

Photo No. 71

Photo No. 72

Photo No. 73

Photo No. 74

Placing the Fingers on the Cello

1. The fingers should be placed on the cello so that the little finger is practically straight and at right angles to the string. The fingers should be arched. (Photo 75)

2. The left thumb is slightly curved but does not exert pressure on the neck. The tip of the thumb is placed opposite or behind the second finger.

3. In the "extended" position the 4th finger is still straight, the thumb always following the second finger and remaining opposite to it. For the backward extension such as playing Bb on the A string, the first position of the 2nd, 3rd and 4th fingers is not altered. The 4th finger is the guide and remains at right angles to the string. It is important to avoid any rotation of the hand or slipping of the first finger. (Photo 76)

Photo No. 75

Photo No. 76

Bass Supplement
The Basics —
Two Versions

Holding the Bass Bow (French)
As posed by Dr. Lucas Drew

1. Hold the bow at the middle, with your left hand, the hair facing the floor, and the tip of the bow pointing toward the left. Photo 77.

Wiggle the right thumb vigorously and then relax the hand.

3. Bend or arch the right thumb and place the right side of the tip of the thumb on the edge of the frog, in such a way that ¼" of the side of the tip is on the stick itself; ¼" is on the frog, and a portion of the left side of the tip of the thumb is free and not in contact with the frog. Photo 78.

4. Place the second finger (or middle finger) over the stick so that the bow contacts the finger slightly above the first crease. The second finger may have two points of contact on the stick, the ferrul and the stick itself. The second finger must always be opposite the thumb. Photo 79.

5. The 3rd finger is placed naturally as we see it in Photo 79.

6. The tip of the little finger comes over the stick covering the little pearl, or slightly above it, with a straight line between the elbow and the top of the hand.

7. Place the first finger on the stick, extending it slightly. It contacts the stick midway between the first and second joints. Notice the difference between the fingers in these positions. Hold this position to the count of ten. Release the bow grip. Now hold the bow again, going through the above steps. Do this a few times.

Photo No. 77

Photo No. 78

Photo No. 79

How to Stand

Stand with your feet about twelve inches apart with the tip of the left foot about four to six inches forward from the tip of the right foot.

Photo No. 80

Balance your weight evenly between both legs. Transfer your weight gently back and forth from one leg to another to memorize the sensation of the natural distribution of body weight. Photo 80.

Holding the Bass and Drawing the Bow

Photo 81 shows us the correct height of the bass. Stand in front of the bass, holding it completely vertical. Drop your right arm with fingers extended. See that the first joint of the first finger touches the bridge. Adjust the end pin of the bass so that this becomes possible.

In Photo 82 we see the bass in playing position. Note that the nut is even with or slightly above the left eyebrow.

Photos 83 and 84 show how we actually hold the bass. Note three important things: 1) that a triangle is formed by the end pin and the toes of each foot; 2) that the right rear edge of the bass touches the left groin; 3) that the inside part of the left knee touches the lower wing of the bass.

Photo No. 81

Photo No. 82

Photo No. 83

Photo No. 84

In Photo 85 we see the placement of the bow at the frog; Photo 86, the placement of the bow at the middle; and in Photo 87 the placement of the bow at the tip.

Make sure that the bow is parallel with the bridge at all times. Note also the natural curvature of the fingers as they hold the bow. At the tip there is almost a straight line from the forearm to the top of the hand. While the arm is practically straight, the elbow must not be in a locked position. There must always be a slight obtuse angle betwen the upper arm and the lower arm. The weight of the arm is carried through the entire movement of the stroke from frog to tip.

On the G and D strings, tilt the stick slightly towards the fingerboard. On the A and E strings it is best to use the full width of the hair. In Photo 88 take particular note of the distances between the fingers. There should be practically an equal distance between the 1st and 2nd fingers, and the 2nd and 4th fingers.

In Photo 89 study the position of the left thumb. It is slightly arched. Also note that it is quite perpendicular and placed in the center of the neck. The important thing is to make sure that it always remains behind or opposite the second finger. The left elbow should be held approximately as high as the tip of the little finger.

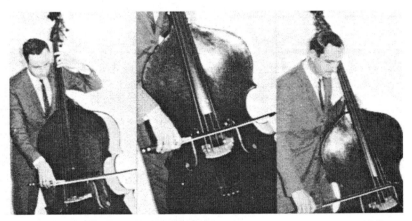

Photo No. 85   **Photo No. 86**   **Photo No. 87**

Photo No. 88   **Photo No. 89**

Holding the Bass Bow (German-Underhand Hold; Dragonetti Bow)
As posed by Frederick Zimmermann

1. (Photo 90) Extend the right hand normally with the thumb slightly raised. Place the nut of the bow into the web between the first finger and the thumb. Flex the thumb so that the flesh part of the thumb lies flat on the stick with the thumb slightly bent outward.

2. Curl the little finger, placing it under the frog so that the inner side of the little finger acts as a shelf for the frog. The bow is now balanced between the thumb and the little finger.

3. There must be a space of about ¾" which will separate the frog from the palm of the hand. This space is important in order to allow the frog of the bow to move freely into the palm and to be released from the palm for the performance of specific bowings.

4. The tips of the 1st and 2nd fingers are placed against the side of the bow away from the palm and must be slightly curved. (Photo 91) They function to exert pressure on the side of the bow, bending the stick toward the fingerboard. At this point this is very similar to holding a pencil.

5. The 3rd finger is placed in the inner groove of the frog at the outer side of the first joint (toward the little finger) exerting pressure downward toward the hair. To summarize, the and 3rd finger exert pressure downward toward the hair. The 1st and 2nd fingers exert pressure on the side of the fingerboard and away from the bridge (Photo 91)

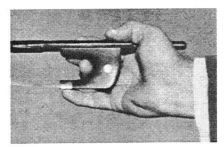

Photo No. 90

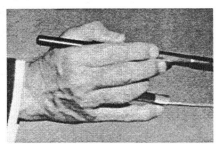

Photo No. 91

Holding the Bass Bow (French-Overhand Hold; Bottesini Bow)

1. At the frog there is almost a straight line from the forearm to the top of the hand. Place the right side of the tip of the thumb on the edge of the frog. The middle finger is opposite the thumb, the bow contacting the finger in the first crease. The same can be said of the third finger. (Photo 92)

2. The tip of the little finger comes over the stick practically covering the little pearl button with a straight line between the elbow and the top of the hand (Photo 93)

3. The right hand side of the tip of the thumb is placed on the edge of the frog so that about ¼" of the side of the tip is on the stick itself, ¼" is on the frog and a portion of the left side of the tip of the thumb is free and not in contact with the frog. (Photo 92)

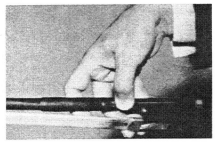

Photo No. 92

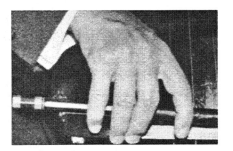

Photo No. 93

How to Hold the Bass

1. The player stands with his full weight on his right leg and right hip. Keep the body erect so that the right leg is in a vertical position.

2. The heel of the left foot is placed about 12″ from the right foot and at an oblique angle. The left knee touches the lower wing of the back of the bass so as to support the bass.

3. The bass must always be brought to the player so that it leans toward the player. (Photo 94) The player should never walk up to the bass.

4. The lower corner of the back of the bass rests against the inner portion of the knee. The thumb is placed on the right hand side of the neck, slightly flexed, between the first and second fingers.

5. The four fingers are placed on the string so that they are flexed and inclined slightly downward. (Photo 95)

6. In the first three or four positions the fleshy parts of the cushions of the fingers are in contact with the strings. It is only in the higher positions that the finger tips come in contact with the strings.

7. At all times the fingers must be flexed and never inward.

8. The fingers never touch. The first, second and fourth fingers must be spaced a half tone apart.

Photo No. 94

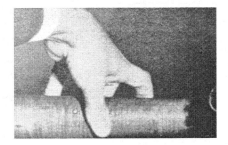

Photo No. 95

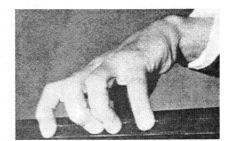

Photo No. 96

How to Draw the Bow

1. Place the bow on the string about two or three inches from the ferule (the metal semi-circular band that secures the hair next to the frog) and about five inches from the bridge. (Photo 96)

2. On the E and A strings the stick is directly above the hair and at right angles to the string.

3. On the D and G strings the stick is tilted toward the fingerboard.

4. Before drawing the first stroke, attention must be focused on the fact that a sufficient amount of weight or pressure is placed on the bow.

5. This pressure is produced with the French bow by a combination of thumb, 1st, 2nd and 3rd fingers acting on the stick with the weight of the arm applied to the hand. The weight of the arm is carried through the entire movement of the stroke from frog to tip. It is advisable at the beginning to hesitate between each stroke so that these steps may be repeated at each end of the bow.

6. With both methods of holding the bow the same volume of tone must be maintained as the player draws nearer to the tip.

A Suggested Well-Balanced Program for String Teaching

The following recommended program contains publications written and/or transcribed by Samuel Applebaum:

FIRST POSITION - ELEMENTARY VIOLIN

METHODS (for string class and individual use, available also for viola, cello, and bass with piano accompaniment)

> Belwin String Builder - Book I
> Applebaum String Course - Book I
> Applebaum - The Young String Student

ETUDES (available also for viola, cello, and bass, with piano acc.)

> Early Etudes
> Etudes for Technic and Musicianship - Book I
> Building Technic with Beautiful Music - Book I

CHAMBER MUSIC (available also for and interchangeable with violas, cellos, and basses)

> Duets for Strings - Book I
> Chamber Music for Two String Instruments - Book I
>   (with piano acc.)

CELLO SOLOS with piano accompaniment

Come to the Sea . . . . Italian Folk Song
Two French Folk Songs . . . . Traditional
In the Swiss Alps . . . . DeBeriot
A Country Scene . . . . Sitt
Minuet . . . . Bach
Rondo. . . . . E. Wagner
To a Wild Rose . . . . MacDowell
Building Technic with Beautiful Music - Book I (collection)
Beautiful Music to Learn by Rote - Book I (collection)

BASS SOLOS with piano accompaniment

Bass Fiddle Waltz . . . . Beyer
Two Jovial Dances . . . . Kingman
Stately Dance . . . . Hassler
March of the Giants . . . . Brian
Pomp and Circumstance . . . . Elgar
Sarabande . . . . Handel
To a Wild Rose . . . . MacDowell
Building Technic with Beautiful Music - Book I (collection)
Beautiful Music to Learn by Rote - Book I (collection)

FIRST POSITION - MEDIUM

METHODS

Belwin String Builder - Book II
Applebaum String Course - Book II

ETUDES and SCALES

First Position Etudes
Etudes for Technic and Musicianship - Book II
Building Technic with Beautiful Music - Book II
Scales for Strings - Book I

CHAMBER MUSIC

Duets for Strings - Book II
Chamber Music for Two String Instruments - Book II
    (with piano acc.)
Beautiful Music for Two String Instruments - Book I and II
    (with piano acc.)

VIOLIN SOLOS with piano accompaniment

In May ....Behr
Smooth Sailing..................................Konrad
The Space Waltz ....Streabbog
Blue Danube Waltz ....Strauss
Kiss Me Again ....Herbert
Dance of the Clowns ....Beyer
To a Wild Rose ....MacDowell
Building Technic with Beautiful Music - Book I (collection)
Beautiful Music to Learn by Rote - Book I (collection)

VIOLA SOLOS with piano accompaniment

Serenade ....DeBeriot
A Graceful Waltz ....P. Isaac
To A Wild Rose...............................MacDowell
Three Waltzes ....Beyer
Grandfather's Clock ....Work
The Country Fair ....Gurlitt
Building Technic with Beautiful Music - Book I (collection)
Beautiful Music to Learn by Rote - Book I (collection)

VIOLIN SOLOS with piano accompaniment

Carnival.......................................Couperin
Whispering Hope ....Hawthorne
Chop Sticks...................................Traditional
Polka ....Dancla
Hobgoblin Dance ....Biehl
Along the Brook ....Lichner
Rigadon ....Peter Lee of Putney
Wedding of the Winds.........................Hall
Little French Boy ....Senaille
Day with the Gypsies.........................Behr
Gavotte ....Sitt
While Strolling Through the Park One Day ....Traditional

Theme and Variations . . . . Papini
Caissons Go Rolling Along . . . . Gruber
Rondo . . . . Mozart
The Little Princess . . . . Hook
Lily . . . . Lichner
Marche Militaire . . . . Schubert
Gertrude's Dream Waltz . . . . Beethoven
Tulip . . . . Lichner
Gypsy Dance . . . . Lichner
Minute Waltz, Op. 64, No. 1 . . . . Chopin
Spanish Dance, Op. 12, No. 1 . . . . Moszkowski
Building Technic with Beautiful Music - Book II (collection)
Beautiful Music to Learn by Rote - Book II (collection)
Twenty Progressive Violin Solos . . . . Applebaum

VIOLA SOLOS with piano accompaniment

Souvenir . . . . Bloch
Sonatina in C . . . . Viguerie
Three Minuets . . . . Handel
Waves at Play . . . . Streabbog
Sonatina . . . . Clementi
To a Wild Rose . . . . MacDowell
Carnival . . . . Couperin
Whispering Hope . . . . Hawthorne
Chop Sticks . . . . Traditional
Polka . . . . Dancla
Hobgoblin Dance . . . . Biehl
Along the Brook . . . . Lichner
Rigadon . . . . Peter Lee of Putney
Wedding of the Winds . . . . Hall
Little French Boy . . . . Senaille
Day with the Gypsies . . . . Behr
Gavotte . . . . Sitt
While Strolling Through the Park One Day . . . . Traditional
Theme and Variations . . . . Papini
Caissons Go Rolling Along . . . . Gruber
Rondo . . . . Mozart
The Little Princess . . . . Hook
Lily . . . . Lichner
Marche Militaire . . . . Schubert
Gertrude's Dream Waltz . . . . Beethoven
Tulip . . . . Lichner
Gypsy Dance . . . . Lichner
Minute Waltz, Op. 64, No. 1 . . . . Chopin
Spanish Dance, Op. 12, No.1 . . . . Moszkowski
Building Technic with Beautiful Music - Book II (collection)
Beautiful Music to Learn by Rote - Book II (collection)
Twenty Progressive Viola Solos . . . . Applebaum

CELLO SOLOS with piano accompaniment

Valse Bluette . . . . Duvernoy
Rondo . . . . Clementi
Sonatina in G . . . . Beethoven

Minuet . . . . J. S. Bach
Petit Valse Brillante . . . . Legye
Three German Dances. . . . . Beethoven
Carnival. . . . . Couperin
Whispering Hope . . . . Hawthorne
Chop Sticks. . . . . Traditional
Polka . . . . Dancla
Hobgoblin Dance . . . . Biehl
Along the Brook . . . . Lichner
Rigadon . . . . Peter Lee of Putney
Wedding of the Winds. . . . . Hall
Little French Boy . . . . Senaille
Day with the Gypsies . . . . Behr
Gavotte . . . . Sitt
While Strolling Through the Park One Day . . . . Traditional
Theme and Variations . . . . Papini
Caissons Go Rolling Along . . . . Gruber
Rondo. . . . . Mozart
The Little Princess . . . . Hook
Lily . . . . Lichner
Marche Militaire . . . . Schubert
Gertrude's Dream Waltz . . . . Beethoven
Tulip. . . . . Lichner
Gypsy Dance . . . . Lichner
Minute Waltz, Op. 64, No. 1 . . . . Chopin
Spanish Dance, Op. 12, No. 1 . . . . Moszkowski
Building Technic with Beautiful Music - Book II (collection)
Beautiful Music to Learn by Rote - Book II (collection)
Twenty Progressive Cello Solos . . . . Applebaum

BASS SOLOS with piano accompaniment

Two Austrian Folk Tunes . . . . Kohler
Gavotte in Rondo Form . . . . Dandrien
Dance of the Wooden Soldiers . . . . Lichner
First Sonatina . . . . L. Drew
Minuet . . . . Pleyel
Carnival. . . . . Couperin
Whispering Hope . . . . Hawthorne
Chop Sticks. . . . . Traditional
Polka . . . . Dancla
Hobgoblin Dance . . . . Biehl
Along the Brook . . . . Lichner
Rigadon . . . . Peter Lee of Putney
Wedding of the Winds. . . . . Hall
Little French Boy . . . . Senaille
Day with the Gypsies . . . . Behr
Gavotte . . . . Sitt
While Strolling Through the Park One Day . . . . Traditional
Theme and Variations . . . . Papini
Caissons Go Rolling Along . . . . Gruber
Rondo. . . . . Mozart
The Little Princess . . . . Hook

Lily . . . . .Lichner
Marche Militaire . . . . .Schubert
Gertrude's Dream Waltz . . . . .Beethoven
Tulip . . . . .Lichner
Gypsy Dance . . . . .Lichner
Minute Waltz, Op. 64, No. 1 . . . . .Chopin
Spanish Dance, Op. 12, No.1 . . . . .Moszkowski
Building Technic with Beautiful Music - Book II (collection)
Beautiful Music to Learn by Rote - Book II (collection)
Twenty Progressive Viola Solos . . . . .Applebaum

THIRD POSITION

METHODS

Belwin String Builder - Book II and III
Applebaum String Course - Book II and III

ETUDES and SCALES

Etudes for Technic and Musicianship - Book II and III
Building Technic with Beautiful Music - Book II and III
Scales for Strings - Book I and II
Orchestral Bowing Etudes

CHAMBER MUSIC

Duets for Strings - Book II and III
Chamber Music for Two String Instruments - Book III
Beautiful Music for Two String Instruments - Book III

VIOLIN SOLOS with piano accompaniment

The Four Pipers . . . . .Destouches
Ninette at Court . . . . .Saint Amans
Bouree . . . . .J. S. Bach
Hungarian Suite . . . . .Bartok
The Rain . . . . .Bohm
Elves Dance . . . . .Bohm
Two Guitars . . . . .Traditional
Allegro . . . . .Vivaldi
Building Technic with Beautiful Music - Book III (collection)

VIOLA SOLOS with piano accompaniment

Sonatina . . . . .Hook
Fantasia (La Cenerentola) . . . . .Dancla
Rigadon in D Minor . . . . .Rameau
Valse Bluette . . . . .Drigo
Spring Song . . . . .Schmitt
Introduction and Polonaise .Bohm
Building Technic with Beautiful Music - Book III (collection)

CELLO SOLOS with piano accompaniment (first four positions)

Intermezzo . . . . .Hook
Sonata in G . . . . .Hook
Andante . . . . .Mozart
Fantasia, Op. 86, No. 1 . . . . .Dancla

Gavotte . . . . .J. S. Bach
Theme and Variations . . . . .Dancla
Building Technic with Beautiful Music - Book III (collection)

BASS SOLOS with piano accompaniment (first five positions)

Minuet in C. . . . . .Pleyel
March. . . . . .Clark
Strange Men . . . . .Schumann
Two Classical Pieces . . . . .Reinagle
Second Sonatina . . . . .L. Drew
Adagio and Allegro . . . . .Galliard
Building Technic with Beautiful Music - Book III (collection)

THE FIRST FIVE POSITIONS

METHODS (available for Violin, Viola, Cello, and Bass)
> The Third and Fifth String Builder
> The Second and Fourth Position String Builder
> The University String Builder (the adult approach)

ETUDES
> Building Technic with Beautiful Music - Book IV

CHAMBER MUSIC
> Beautiful Music for Two String Instruments - Book IV

SOLOS
> Building Technic with Beautiful Music - Book IV (collection)

THE FIRST SEVEN POSITIONS

METHODS (available for Violin, Viola, Cello, and Bass)
> The Best of Sevcik - Book I (developing skills in the positions)

ALL THE POSITIONS

METHODS (available for Violin, Viola, Cello, and Bass)
> The Best of Sevcik - Book II (developing shifting skills with all the bowing styles)

MUSIC FOR STRING ORCHESTRA - COLLECTIONS
> (may be used for string quartet or any
> combination of strings with piano)

FIRST POSITION - ELEMENTARY

> First Program for Strings
> Chamber Music for Strings - Book I
> Away We Go

FIRST POSITION - MEDIUM

> Flying High
> Concert Program for String Orchestra
> Chamber Music for Strings - Book II
> Adventures in Orchestra (with James Ployhar)
> Happy Sounds for Orchestra (with James Ployhar)

FIRST THREE POSITIONS

> Orchestral Holiday (with James Ployhar)
> Beautiful Music for Orchestra (with James Ployhar)
> Christmas Strings (with Louis Gordon)

FIRST FIVE POSITIONS

> Orchestral Moods (with James Ployhar)

MUSIC FOR STRING QUARTET/STRING ORCHESTRA

The Best of Haydn .... with Paul Paradise
The Best of Mozart .... with Paul Paradise

MUSIC FOR STRING ORCHESTRA - SINGLE SELECTIONS

FIRST THREE POSITIONS

To a Wild Rose .... E. MacDowell
Theme and Variations .... G. Papini
Gypsy Dance .... H. Lichner
Sonatina for Strings .... M. Clementi
Serenade for Strings .... W. A. Mozart
Ninette at Court .... Saint Amans
Air Varie, Op. 89, No. 5 .... C. Dancla
Minute for Strings .... G. F. Handel
Two Hungarian Tunes .... B. Bartok
Sarabande .... Carl Bohm
Garden Dance .... G. Vargas
Nola .... F. Arndt
Moods .... B. Bartok
Siciliano and Allegro .... J. Galliard
Postcards from Mexico .... Louis Gordon
Western Sketches .... Louis Gordon
Sleigh Ride .... Leroy Anderson
The Syncopated Clock .... Leroy Anderson
The Little Drummer Boy .... Davis, Onorati, Simeone

An American Suite . . . . .Bruce Chase
English Folk Song Suite . . . . .Charles B. Jones
Lady of Spain . . . . .T. Evans
Prelude and Fugue . . . . .Louis Gordon
A Tribute to John Philip Sousa . . . . .arr. Applebaum
A Handel Suite . . . . .Gordon/arr. Applebaum
A Bach Suite . . . . .arr. Applebaum

FOR ADVANCED PLAYERS

Man of LaMancha . . . . .Darion-Gordon
Fiddle-Faddle . . . . .Leroy Anderson
Chamber Suite in D .G. F. Handel
Mazurka . . . . .E. Mlynarski
Concerto in A Minor (1st Mvt.) . . . . .J. S. Bach
Divertimento for Strings . . . . .Ira Schwarz
Essay for Strings . . . . .Walter Chorssen

MUSIC FOR FULL ORCHESTRA - COLLECTIONS

FIRST POSITION

Adventures in Orchestra (with James Ployhar)
Orchestral Holiday (with James Ployhar)
Happy Sounds for Orchestra (with James Ployhar)

FIRST THREE POSITIONS

Orchestral Moods (with James Ployhar)

FIRST FIVE POSITIONS

Beautiful Music for Orchestra (with James Ployhar)

MUSIC FOR FULL ORCHESTRA - SINGLE SELECTIONS

Concerto in A Minor (1st Mvt.) . . . . .J. S. Bach
(with Louis Gordon)

The following are selected string publications available from Alfred Publishing:

STRING METHODS

Learn to Play a Stringed Instrument -
  Book I, II, and III . . . . .Matesky and Womack
Well-Tempered String Player . . . . .Matesky
Think Strings (violin) . . . . .Pezzano and Meneely

BEGINNING STRING FOLIOS

Learn to Play in the Orchestra -
Book I and II . . . . .Matesky

VIOLIN SOLOS

Concertino for Violin . . . . .Matesky
Mozartino for Violin . . . . .Matesky

MUSIC FOR FULL ORCHESTRA - SINGLE SELECTIONS

African Trilogy . . . . .Diamond/Gold
Airs from "The Beggar's Opera" . . . . .Gay/Gordon
Appalachian Festival . . . . .arr. Gordon
Bach in Rock . . . . .Feldstein
Ballet from the Opera "William Tell" . . . . .Rossini/Gordon
Baroque Dance Suite . . . . .Gordon
Bartók Rock . . . . .Feldstein
Beautiful Noise (Concert Highlights) . . . . . .Diamond/O'Reilly
Chanukah Celebration (with opt. unison
    chorus) . . . . .arr. Feldstein
Christmas in Concert . . . . .McBeth
Double String Romp . . . . .Hastings
Folk Baroque Suite . . . . .Palmer/Hastings
Heather's Theme . . . . .O'Reilly
Highlights from Jonathan Livingston
    Seagull . . . . .Diamond/O'Reilly
Holly and the Mistletoe, The . . . . .Matesky
Holly Holy . . . . .Diamond/Cacavas
Indian Dances . . . . .Matesky
Jazz Suite for Strings and Rhythm . . . . .Tiffault
Jig-O-Rama . . . . .Matesky
Kabalevskiana . . . . .Hastings
March for Young People . . . . .Shostakovich/Matesky
Midnight Minuet . . . . .Haydn/Klotman
Neil Diamond in Concert . . . . .Diamond/Gold
Orchestral Suite for Old St. Nick . . . . .arr. Feldstein
Pizzicato Rock . . . . .Feldstein
Queen Anne Suite . . . . .Gordon
Rock, Rock, Merrily on High . . . . .Laurett
Rock-A-Bell Jingle . . . . .Hastings
Rockin' Christmas . . . . .arr. Feldstein
Schumannesque . . . . .Hastings
September Morn . . . . .Diamond/O'Reilly
Suite for Strings . . . . .Scheidt/Klotman
Song Sung Blue . . . . .Diamond/Kinyon
Sweet Caroline . . . . .Diamond/Kinyon
Two Classic Dances .Matesky
Two Mozart Melodies . . . . .Gordon
Variations on a Famous Theme
    by Paganini . . . . .Matesky
Variations on a Theme by Beethoven . . . . . .Matesky
You Don't Bring Me Flowers . . . . .Diamond/Forbes
You Don't Bring Me Flowers . . . . .Diamond/O'Reilly

An Abridged List of Suggested Readings

BOOKS

Applebaum, Samuel and Sada. *The Way They Play.* Vols. 1, 2, 3.

Applebaum, Samuel and Branigan, Alan. *The Way They Play.* Vols. 4, 5.

Applebaum, Samuel and Roth, Henry. *The Way They Play.* Vols. 6, 7, 8, 9, 10.

Auer, Leopold. *Violin Playing As I Teach It.*

Bachman, Albert. *An Encyclopedia of the Violin.*

Barrett, Henry. *The Viola.*

Barjansky, Serge. *The Physical Basis of Tone Production.*

Benfield, Warren. *The Art of Bass Playing.*

Bloch, A. *How to Practice.*

Boyden, David O. *The History of Violin Playing from Its Origins to 1761.*

Bostelman, Louis J. *An Analysis of Violin Practice.*

Broadley, Arthur. *Chats to Cello Students.*

Bronstein, R. *The Science of Violin Playing.*

Bytovetski, Paul L. *How to Master the Violin.*

Camplell, Margaret. *The Great Violinists.*

Carabo - Cone. *Concepts for Strings.*

Cook, Clifford A. *String Teaching and Some Related Topics.*

Cook, Clifford A. *Suzuki Education in Action.*

Courvoisier, Karl. *The Technics of Violin Playing.*

Dannemann, Ulrich. *Violin Teaching.*

Dillon, Jacquelyn and Kriechbaum, Casimir B., Jr. *How to Design and Teach a Successful School String Orchestra Program.*

Eisenberg, M. *Cello Playing of Today.*

Flesch, Carl. *The Art of Violin Playing.*

Flesch, Carl. *Urstudien.*

Flesch, Carl. *Violin Fingering.*

Flesch, Carl. *The Violinists Handbook.*

Geminiani, Francesco. *The Art of Playing on the Violin.*

Green, Barry. *Advanced Techniques of Double Bass Playing.*

Green, Barry. *The Fundamentals of Double Bass Playing.*

Green, E. A. *Orchestral Bowing.*

Grodner, Murray. *Literature of the Double Bass.*

Gruenberg, Eugene. *Violin Teaching and Violin Study.*

Havas, Kato. *The Twelve Lesson Course.*

Henkle, Ted. *The String Teacher's Handbook.*

Hodgson, Percival. *Motion Study and Violin Bowing.*

Kneisel, F. *Principles of Bowing and Phrasing.*

Krasner, Louis. *String Problems.*

Kuhn, W. *Principles of String Class Teaching.*

Kuhn, W. *The Strings.*

Lehmann, G. *The Violinists' Lexicon.*

Lochner, Louis. *Fritz Kreisler.*

Loft, Abram. *Violin and Keyboard the Duo Repertoire,* Vols. 1, 2.

Martens, Ferderick H. *String Mastery.*

Matz, R. - Aronson, L. *The Complete Cellist.*

Menuhin, Yehudi. *Six Lessons with Yehudi Menuhin.*

Mills, E. *In the Suzuki Style.*

Mozart, Leopold. *A Treatise on the Fundamental Principles of Violin Playing.*

Neumann, F. *Ornamentation in Baroque and Post-Baroque Music.*

Neumann, F. *Violin Left Hand Technique.*

Pernecky, J. *Basic Guide to Violin Playing.*
Potter, Louis. *The Art of Cello Playing.*
Riley, Maurice *The History of the Viola.*
Rolland, Paul. *Basic Principles of Violin Playing.*
Rolland, Paul. *Prelude to String Playing.*
Rosenberg, Fred. *The Violin - The Technic of Relaxation and Power.*
Roth, Henry. *Master Violinists in Performance.*
Seagrave, Barbara G. and Berman, Joel. *Dictionary of Bowing Terms.*
Shapiro, H. M. *The Physical Approach to Violinistic Problems.*
Starker, Janos. *An Organized Method of String Playing.*
Starr, William. *The Suzuki Violinist.*
Stoeving, P. *Master of the Bow.*
Szigeti, Joseph. *Szigeti on the Violin.*
Taper, Bernard. *Cellist in Exile.* (a portrait of Pablo Casals)
Tertis, Lionel. *Beauty of Tone in String Playing.*
Thistleton, F. *Modern Viola Technique.*
Timerman, H. *How to Produce a Beautiful Tone on the Violin.*
Tortelier, Paul. *How I Play - How I Teach.*
Waller, G. R. *Virbrato Method.*
Whone, Herbert. *The Simplicity of Playing the Violin.*
Winn, Edith. *First Steps in Violin Playing.*
Winn, Edith. *How to Prepare for Kreutzer.*
Winn, Edith. *How to Study Fiorillo.*
Winn, Edith. *How to Study Rode.*
Winn, Edith. *How to Study Gavinies.*
Yampolski, I. M. *The Principles of Violin Fingering.*
Yost, Phyllis. *Playing the String Games.*
Zimmermann, Frederick, *A Contemporary Concept of Bowing Technique for the Double Bass.*

FILMS

The Samuel Applebaum String Method —

An audio-visual teaching supplement to the printed, detailed, and illustrated method. (16mm, color)
Belwin-Mills/Columbia Pictures, Hialeah, Florida 33014

The Violin —

Film One: Left-hand technique
Film Two: Right-hand technique
16 mm, 33 in. each
Film Manual (covers all units)
The Bureau of Audio-Visual Instruction
P. O. Box 2093
Madison, Wisconsin 53701

RECORDINGS

SAMUEL APPLEBAUM RECORDING TECHNIQUE AND MUSICIANSHIP SIMULTANEOUSLY
No. CR-1028
(2-Album Set)

THE COMPLETE SERIES INCLUDES:

CR-1020
THE STRING BOWINGS
(How and when to teach them)
2-album set

CR-1021
HOW TO DEVELOP A BEAUTIFUL VIBRATO

CR-1022
HOW TO RAISE THE STANDARDS OF STRING CLASS TEACHING
(A series of basic special studies)

CR-1023
HOW AND WHEN TO INTRODUCE ROTE PROJECTS IN STRING TEACHING

CR-1024
HOW TO DEVELOP A BASIC LEFT HAND TECHNIQUE

CR-1025
HOW TO DEVELOP A BEAUTIFUL TONE
(The science and art of tone production)

CR-1026
HOW TO LOSE YOUR FEAR OF THE UPPER POSITIONS
(Specific Exercises)

CR-1027
SIXTEEN BASIC PRINCIPLES OF GENERAL MUSICIANSHIP
(An aid to interpreting music)
2-album set

GOLDEN CREST RECORDS, INC.
P.O. Box 2859, 220 Broadway
Huntington Station, New York 11746